MW01034844

PRAISE FOR
FIND YOUR FIGHT

"If you want to be an activist for human dignity and a better world, and not just a bystander lamenting the course of global, national, or local issues, this book will stimulate and guide you. As Ruderman warns, there are no 'quick fixes.' Activism is a marathon, not a sprint, and progress rarely happens in a straight line. A timely and well-written book, especially for a youthful activist with conviction."

—Tom Harkin, former United States Senator from Iowa

"Jay Ruderman's book is a guidebook with a formula to inspire each and every one of us *to make a difference* in life. Jay writes from personal experience, sharing with us that it can be done. Read the book, take it to heart, and you, too, can make a difference."

—Abraham Foxman, National Director
Emeritus of the Anti-Defamation League (ADL)

"*Find Your Fight* is an essential guide for those wanting to learn more about what it means to be an activist. Jay Ruderman provides practical steps that anyone can use to better their efforts as an ally for the issues they're passionate about."

—Marlee Matlin, Academy Award®-
winning actress, director, and activist

"In a world where there is so much need for change, we are lacking the tools we need to truly make a difference. Jay Ruderman has done the work and provides clear guidance that will inspire those looking to make a real impact."

—**Jim Langevin,** former member of Congress from Rhode Island

"In *Find Your Fight*, Jay Ruderman offers hope, courage, and inspiration. With practical lessons and success stories, this book is guaranteed to empower both experienced activists and those looking for a place to start."

—**Tony Coelho,** former Majority Whip of the United States House of Representatives

"*Find Your Fight* will leave you energized to take real action and equip you with the tools you need to do it. You will hear from those who have been there and learn how to be an activist and advocate in an effective way."

—**Geena Davis,** Academy Award®-winning actress and activist

"If you are looking to effect change but feel lost on exactly how, *Find Your Fight* will help guide your way. Jay Ruderman offers his experience, knowledge, and passion to make sure you have what you need to step up for your cause."

—**Julianna Margulies,** Emmy Award®-winning actress

"Jay Ruderman has a secret he wants to share with the rest of us: there is nothing to stop you from correcting an injustice, reducing inequity, and righting a wrong, if you'll only dedicate yourself to getting it done. Through years of experience working for those with disabilities, Jay has picked up hard-earned lessons that he wants all of us to know about. Read this compelling book to learn why it's possible for each one of us to make the world a better place."

—**Judy Woodruff,** former anchor of the *PBS NewsHour*

"If you're looking to effect change and make a difference in your community, but feel unsure where to start, *Find Your Fight* is the spark you need to ignite your journey. Jay Ruderman offers his unique experience, vast knowledge, and unwavering passion to equip you to become a change agent."

—**Tiffany Smith-Anoa'i,** Executive Vice President
of Entertainment Diversity, Inclusion,
and Communications at Paramount Global

"To his laurels as a celebrated philanthropist and activist, Jay Ruderman now adds the title of inspirational author. *Find Your Fight* is a lively and practical handbook exemplifying the rule that the most important lessons are the products of experience. Jay's insights on persistence, diligence, and community-building will be invaluable to anyone with a passion for improving the world."

—**Joseph Aoun,** President of Northeastern University

"*Find Your Fight* is an essential playbook for anyone who wants to create change in the world."

—**Peter Farrelly,** Academy Award®-winning director

"Jay Ruderman has written a thoughtful, compelling, and enjoyable guide to making positive, lasting change. This book is perfect for anyone seeking actionable strategies and inspiring stories to turn their passion into a powerful force for good."

—**Bill Kramer,** CEO, Academy of Motion Picture Arts and Sciences

"Jay Ruderman has devoted his life to creating a better world. This inspiring book provides real, practical advice on how you, too, can make a difference in the communities in which you live and work. It is also an engaging and honest read that draws on some of Jay's own personal experiences."

—**Ronald Liebowitz,** President Emeritus of Brandeis University

"There are so many people everywhere who would love to contribute to positive change, make the world a better place. Few of us, however, know how and where to start. Jay Ruderman has made it his life's work. *Find Your Fight* spells out exactly what it takes to be the change you want to see in the world."

—**Bobby Farrelly,** PGA Award®-winning
producer and American film director

"Jay Ruderman has been the driver of a model for activism to right wrongs and help people. Now he has taken the lessons he has learned from decades on the front lines and put them into a manual for those wanting to join the fight and help heal the world. The book weaves together compelling stories from Ruderman's life and work and many he has encountered to provide guideposts and advice for the next generation of activists."

—**Norm Ornstein,** Emeritus Scholar, the American
Enterprise Institute; Vice President of the Matthew
Harris Ornstein Memorial Foundation

Foreword by **OCTAVIA SPENCER**
Academy Award®-winning actress and activist

FIND YOUR
FIGHT

Make Your Voice
Heard for the Causes
that Matter Most

JAY RUDERMAN

GREENLEAF
BOOK GROUP PRESS

Published by Greenleaf Book Group Press
Austin, Texas
www.gbgpress.com

Distributed by Greenleaf Book Group

For ordering information or special discounts for bulk purchases, please contact Greenleaf Book Group at PO Box 91869, Austin, TX 78709, 512.891.6100.

Cover design by Greenleaf Book Group and Kate Wimbiscus Sievers
Design and composition by Greenleaf Book Group and Mimi Bark

Publisher's Cataloging-in-Publication data is available.

Print ISBN: 978-1-963827-07-1

eBook ISBN: 978-1-963827-08-8

To offset the number of trees consumed in the printing of our books, Greenleaf donates a portion of the proceeds from each printing to the Arbor Day Foundation. Greenleaf Book Group has replaced over 50,000 trees since 2007.

Printed in the United States of America on acid-free paper

25 26 27 28 29 30 31 32   10 9 8 7 6 5 4 3 2 1

First Edition

To Shira, for your love, guidance, and support

*To Michael, Tamar, Yehonatan, and Ariel, I hope the lessons
in this book will be meaningful for your lives*

*To my parents, Morton z'l and Marcia, and to my siblings,
Sharon and Todd, for always being there for me*

CONTENTS

FOREWORD

First Lady Eleanor Roosevelt once said, "We do not have to become heroes overnight, just a step at a time." And therein lies the value of this book: It outlines the steps one must take as an activist to achieve change. It gives activists at any stage in their journey a blueprint to be impactful, or more impactful, in the service of their cause. I've seen these methods work to bring about much-needed change in my own industry, and I think your efforts will certainly benefit from them as well.

Jay Ruderman is someone I probably never would have met in my life. We were introduced through Academy Award*-winning director and producer Peter Farrelly to collaborate on Jay's goal to promote disability inclusion and authentic representation in the film and television industry. When Jay first approached me about participating in a public service announcement promoting authentic representation of actors with disabilities, the decision was easy. As someone who grew up seeing too few characters who looked like me on screen, his cause hit close to my heart. Over the years, I've had the opportunity to work alongside him and see how effective he has been in creating change. How exactly has Jay accomplished this? That's where this book comes in.

Reading *Find Your Fight* felt like sitting down with Jay one-on-one and getting a real understanding of how the world of advocacy works. Jay's passion for his cause comes across in the book as he breaks down valuable knowledge about his method and mindset through his advocacy efforts.

For one thing, Jay portrays how activism is never the work of a single individual. Success comes through the combined efforts of many, both in strategic partnerships and in the strength of collective action. In addition, Jay emphasizes the importance of fostering the next generation's potential, something Jay and I closely agree on. In addition to pushing for authentic representation in the film and television industry, my personal fight is to ensure that young people from all backgrounds have the opportunity to receive a quality education. And in a gesture to the importance of community, I've discovered a connection to likeminded activists in Los Angeles through City Year, an organization that helps mentor and support students in local schools. This strong group of young activists will carry on the fight for all groups into the future.

Jay shares in his book that the first step to making change is finding a cause that's close to one's heart and deciding to make a difference. For me, that cause is education because of the value my family always placed on it. And education is something that's shaped my own path in life.

One unique facet of Jay's brand of activism is that sometimes in the quest for creating change, you need to get comfortable courting controversy. In activism, as in life, change does not happen within people's comfort zones. Controversy issues a challenge, draws headlines, and ignites conversations.

So please, read on. The wisdom in the pages that follow will surely help you gain ground in whatever cause is important to you.

—Octavia Spencer
Academy Award°-winning actress, director, producer
Los Angeles, California
2024

INTRODUCTION

This book is a love letter to activism.

There is nothing more fulfilling and meaningful than achieving real change in your community—by challenging unfair systems, taking and defending controversial stands in public, shaking up the conventional wisdom, and ultimately transforming social attitudes.

I know, because I've done it again and again.

My particular brand of activism involves taking an issue and making it bigger, exposing it to the extent that attitudes begin to change. I've done this successfully for years by using the media and entertainment industry—as an outsider—to pretty spectacular effect. I've advocated for multiple causes over the course of my life, primarily around disability rights and mental health. Thanks to my persistent activism and the commitment of my team, our allies, and the disability community, entertainment companies worth hundreds of billions of dollars, including ViacomCBS, NBCUniversal, Paramount Pictures, and Sony Pictures Entertainment have all committed to affirming disability as part of Hollywood's defini-tion of diversity, encouraging auditions of actors with disabilities and authentic representation of disabled characters on film and television.[1]

But even I didn't anticipate the snowball effect of my work: how it would proliferate, involve Hollywood studios as well as celebri-ties, and show itself in the Oscars. In 2020, for the first time, an actor with Down syndrome, Zack Gottsagen, stepped onstage to present an Academy Award. And in 2022, the movie *CODA*, star-ring talented actors who are deaf, scored three Oscars, including Best Picture and Best Actor in a Supporting Role. We've even forged a partnership with the new Academy Museum of Motion Pictures around issues of equity and inclusion.[2] And looking beyond the entertainment industry, I've also led initiatives that made strides in sports, especially Major League Baseball and the Olympics.[3] The impact of this activism has been huge, and it continues to unfold without me.

ANYONE CAN BE AN ACTIVIST

As president of the Ruderman Family Foundation, I've also sup-ported countless organizations and programs and funded millions of dollars in philanthropic projects. But you don't have to be rich or powerful or even connected to be a successful activist. What it takes is challenging attitudes and influencing people by getting like-minded allies to join you. If a quiet, controversy-courting idealist like me, who doesn't even live on the right coast, can make change in a major industry, you too can have a big impact on our world.

So many of us are frustrated with the failures of our social, economic, and political systems—with rampant inequality, environmental degradation, partisan gridlock, and how-is-this-still-happening discrimination and prejudice. We need to believe that we can act, and we can. But let me say this: finding your fight should never be about promoting hatred and violence. Effective activism is about using your voice, not harassment and physical threats, to promote positive movements for peace, justice, fairness, and a better world. There is no role for the destruction of personal property, physical assaults, ad hominem attacks, intimidation, or the denigration of individuals based on their race, nationality, gender, sexual orientation, or religion. I cannot stress that enough. Those who allow hateful emotions to guide their actions compromise their activism and the ideals they stand for.

Successful activism is not about cynically doing "whatever it takes," and it's certainly not about your job title or financial resources. It's about the depth of your commitment to human dignity and a better world. Great promoters of social change include schoolteachers and scientists, lawyers and homemakers, artists and physicians, athletes and politicians, ministers and engineers, students and retirees. Through my popular podcast series *All About Change*, I've spoken with hundreds of people from all walks of life whose circumstances propelled them into activism. They saw a need, they acted, their cause attracted support and resources, and they achieved change.

Activism can be as simple as speaking out. I've often thought of the story of D'Arcee Neal, who lives with cerebral palsy. In October 2015, Neal was returning home (ironically, from a conference about issues related to accessibility for people with disabilities) via a United flight from San Francisco to Washington. The tiny washrooms on airplanes are too difficult for him to use, so when the jet touched down, he waited impatiently for a wheelchair to carry him down the aisle to the terminal restroom. But an airline mix-up led to an extended delay, and Neal was left waiting long after the other passengers had deplaned. Finally, close to a half hour later, he couldn't wait any longer and began an agonizing crawl to the washroom—as airline personnel looked on and did nothing. The next day, United representatives called Neal to apologize and offered him a $300 compensatory payment, which he accepted.[4]

Now, think of all the people who could have intervened to prevent that situation—the flight attendants, the pilot and co-pilot, the ground crew, the person who pushes the wheelchairs in the airport, the leadership of the airline and the airline industry, the people responsible for regulating the industry, lawyers, judges . . . the list goes on. If any of them had been advocates instead of passive bystanders—stepping up to do the right thing and making their voices heard about the problem—it might have resulted in greater impact than a few hundred dollars and an apology. Changing people's perceptions about such basic liberties as having access to a washroom is social activism at its most fundamental level. Opportunities for activism are everywhere.

RULES OF ENGAGEMENT

I'm incredibly proud of the work I've done as an activist, but I'm no celebrity. For the purposes of this book, Hollywood and disability rights are just examples in a larger conversation about activism. They serve to illustrate how very powerful a cultural conversation can be, particularly when it's got an engine like the media and entertainment industry behind it. The #MeToo movement is another great example of this. My rules of engagement are applicable to many other causes and are based on grassroots instead of boardroom activism. As I show in the following chapters, these lessons can help you make a difference, no matter your age, gender, class, area of activism, or level of power and influence.

If I can do it, you can too. I have a results-based formula that works. It's a remarkably effective approach that can be better than philanthropy at protecting and advancing the rights of those often overlooked in our society. Don't get me wrong; philanthropy is definitely important as one means of addressing that pain. No part of me wants to diminish its role in alleviating society's problems. Money is also important, and I'd never claim otherwise. But I've seen firsthand how you can waste a lot of money with little success. All too often, the traditional operations of nonprofit and charitable organizations are shaped by the agendas and attitudes of the rich and powerful—many of whom assume their financial success gives them singular insight into societal issues. I am an activist who is still a philanthropist, but I've broken ranks with the methods of traditional philanthropy by taking and defending controversial stands in public, shaking up the conventional wisdom, and ultimately transforming social attitudes.

I've also learned that you can achieve tremendous success as an activist with very little money. I've seen this over and over again, for example, on social media. If an individual can successfully project their image and message online, they can attract attention, support, and the resources to promote the cause they believe in. It doesn't take money or connections. What it takes is persistence, creativity, hard work, and the ability to get your message across to a wide audience.

The first step is to find your fight. In this book, I explore how to identify an issue you care deeply about that suffers from a lack of leadership spearheading change. I show you why persistence comes first—the ability to keep fighting despite the odds, the anguish, and the inevitable ups and downs of committed activism. I show you how to focus on your issue with preparation and expertise, and how to go from working against the people you've criticized to working with them as an ally to create positive change. I explain how I've tackled big problems by challenging unfair systems. I share inspirational stories of a wide range of activists, of all ages, around the world. And I speak candidly about the events in my life that have shaped my activism or reflect it.

This book is divided into three sections that show how you can successfully create change, from preparation to progress. **Part I: Be Persistent and Be Prepared** explains what it takes to be an effective activist. You have to find a cause that you truly care about. You have to be persistent. And you always have to know your facts.

In **Part II: Speak Out, Spark Controversy, and Grab Attention,** I discuss why you have to create and maintain an advocacy community that can amplify your voice. I explain why controversies are opportunities and how activists can execute effective social pressure campaigns to create change. I also show why it's helpful to ally with well-known advocates to get your message across—and why allying with those you criticize to achieve change is essential.

Finally, in **Part III: Make Progress and Mark Your Progress**, I talk about why it's so important to care for yourself and your community to avoid burnout and to walk away from situations that sap your energy but make little impact. I also emphasize how important it is to celebrate your wins, no matter how small or incremental they may be, and to stay flexible in adapting your message and strategy to new times and tools. Above all, activism isn't a calling that should be endured. It's a passion that should be celebrated and inspire joy.

It has in my life, and I truly hope that it will in yours.

PART 1

BE PERSISTENT
AND BE PREPARED

CHAPTER 1

FIND YOUR FIGHT

"You can speak well if your tongue can
deliver the message of your heart."
—JOHN FORD, **American film director and producer**

As an activist, I don't want people to change their behavior because they're *with* me. Nor do I want them to do it *for* me. I want them to do it because they care about justice and the cause I'm fighting for. And if I'm successful, they will care. They may even develop conviction and take action.

Most people empathize with those who are treated unfairly. And in my experience, you can appeal to their sense of justice by speaking to them, respectfully, from the heart. In advocacy and life, whatever your cause (and no matter how bad the behavior of those who oppose it), I urge you to believe in and see the fairness and goodness in most human beings. That goodness drives our response to injustice and invites others to respond in kind. At the end of the day, I have to believe that we are good and just.

I also believe that when you speak to others from your heart, you have a powerful capacity to move their hearts and minds. Many will want to step up, support you, and take action to make things better. Propelled by your personal passion to make a difference, you can, and you will, create change.

START FROM THE HEART

You have to find your fight—and in activism, the personal is the professional. Personal experience roots this work in a set of values, and it's the strength of those values that keeps you on task, that emboldens you to speak out about an issue when you are afraid to do so, and that comforts you when others criticize your efforts.

In my case, disability rights chose me. Like many people, I have some lived experience with disability. I've suffered in the past from periodic depression, which first reared its head in my thirties and was so severe at one point that I didn't want to eat. My father also developed a disability that severely restricted his mobility, and my son was diagnosed with attention-deficit hyperactivity disorder (ADHD). This is not so unusual; one in four Americans has a disability of some kind. It's an issue that touches all of us, whether directly or by association.

When I first decided to focus on disability rights, I learned that though a quarter of Americans have a disability, only one out of a hundred actors onscreen actually has the disability of the character they portray. In movies, at least historically, we've had lauded performances by Daniel Day-Lewis (*My Left Foot*), Dustin Hoffman (*Rain Man*), and Tom Hanks (*Forrest Gump*) depicting disability, but there hasn't been a lot of authentic representation onscreen. Those roles were affectingly played by able-bodied actors. As a result, a fourth of our population has been nearly invisible when it comes to the influential mediums of television and film and hasn't had the chance for authentic representation in the few roles available in those mediums.

I have always believed that culture is just as powerful as legislation in determining the direction of society—sometimes even more so. And entertainment, especially, influences the hearts and minds of those who consume it, eventually shifting our perceptions and behavior. That's why representation in Hollywood is such a hot-button issue. The *New York Times* called the 2015 #OscarsSoWhite social justice campaign "the hashtag that changed the Oscars." But you don't need to be a movie buff to realize that it also changed the entertainment industry. It paved the way for so many other social justice movements, particularly those focused on the industry's treatment of marginalized groups. And it changed (or is changing) the way we "see" those groups in movies and television. It's changing us.[1]

For example, consider what a non-event it is today to encounter same-sex couples in the media. Then think back to the controversy surrounding the 1997 coming-out episode of the ABC sitcom *Ellen*. It aired at a time when gay characters, if they appeared at all in storylines, occupied minor roles from a playbook of tropes that included the horribly one-dimensional "gay best friend." You can see how far we've come.[2]

As long as our society doesn't backtrack, that's encouraging. And by my reckoning, how far I've come as an activist is encouraging too. Shortly after my father, Mort, asked me to lead the family foundation, we made disability rights one of our focus areas. Disability rights are civil rights, and at the time, the disability community was pushing back against the prevailing segregation-based approach to disabilities. The accepted idea, at least historically, was that society needed to take care of people with disabilities, instead of treating everyone as equals. The disability community was long thought to be best served by segregated programs and facilities, such as sheltered workshops, non-integrated schools, and group homes. Unfortunately, in the past, there had not been enough focus on inclusion, although that was changing. But it still wasn't changing in entertainment and culture, and I wondered why. I realized there was not enough leadership on the issue since actors with disabilities might risk their own careers and opportunities by speaking out. But being an outsider, I wasn't vulnerable to being blackballed, so I decided to go after it.

Our foundation began by deeply researching the issue and publishing our findings in the media. I then began to challenge the status quo by using the media to criticize big-box-office movies for using able-bodied actors to play characters with disabilities. Eventually, I went after celebrities themselves. The response wasn't always pretty, but I'd had some experience with this approach, and I thought I knew what to expect.

I then circulated an open letter calling on studio and network executives to pledge to create more opportunities for people with disabilities and make more inclusive casting decisions. The letter was signed by the likes of George Clooney, Joaquin Phoenix, Glenn Close, and the Farrelly brothers. I also approached studios directly requesting that they commit, in writing, to making auditions accessible to actors with disabilities. Those initiatives generated something of a breakthrough.[3]

Then, noting that those I had challenged were making progress, I changed course. I began to work together as an ally with the very people and organizations I'd criticized. Since I'd put them in the media hot seat, they were more than willing to work with me to improve their image and approach. But our alliance went beyond simple collaboration, because I also launched a way to recognize and reward those new industry partners through a "Seal of Authentic Representation," which itself won media attention.

DECIDE TO MAKE A DIFFERENCE

By finding a fight that moved me, I was able to move others over time. I succeeded in making a tangible difference in the world of entertainment media because my personal commitment propelled me to take risks and actions that attracted support and attention. It's a powerful formula for social impact.

Just ask Chrissy Beckles, who felt driven to help abandoned dogs on the island of Puerto Rico. Chrissy had grown up with animals and had always felt an affinity and connection with them. So, in 2007, when she visited Puerto Rico for the first time, she was shocked to see the huge number of stray dogs with no access to food, fresh water, or veterinary care. Many of them were living lives of severe suffering. Puerto Rico's animal shelter system was drastically overwhelmed, with only five shelters across the island's seventy-eight municipalities, and their euthanasia rate was over 94 percent.

"It is hard to walk on a beach without seeing abandoned dogs—some very cute pups who sometimes chew rocks because they're so hungry," Chrissy recounted when I interviewed her for my podcast, *All About Change.*

> There were abandoned dogs everywhere and a lot of indifference to the animals. There are estimated to be in excess of half a million of them in Puerto Rico, which is roughly the size of the state of Connecticut. So if you think in those terms, if Connecticut had half a million stray dogs running around, it would be front-page news in every newspaper. I was completely, immediately overwhelmed by what I saw.

When Chrissy flew home to New York, she spent the entire plane ride thinking, "What am I going to do? I don't know what it's going to look like, but I know I need to do something. I can't get back to New York and forget what I've seen."

She was working as an advertising and marketing consultant, but she was also a fighter, literally—a champion amateur boxer who had competed in Madison Square Garden three times and had won several titles, including the New York Golden Gloves. She decided to start fighting to help the abandoned dogs of Puerto Rico.

Chrissy started by supporting and volunteering with various rescue organizations. She also adopted a stray dog from Puerto Rico, but she knew that she had to do more. So Chrissy founded the Sato Project, a group that works in the poorest Puerto Rican municipalities to rescue, rehabilitate, adopt, shelter, spay/neuter, and vaccinate abandoned dogs. *Sato* is the colloquial word for stray dog in Puerto Rico, and Chrissy's project focused its efforts on the southeast coast of the island in an area officially named Playa Lucia but nicknamed Dead Dog Beach for all the animals abandoned there. "By concentrating our rescue efforts in one area, specifically on this beach," she explained, "we could visibly and tangibly see the impact that we were having."

When Chrissy first started visiting that beach, she recalled, it was definitely a dumping ground.

> There is no food source on that beach. We found dogs that were not even able to walk. We unequivocally know that someone drove them there and dumped them. There were also extraordinarily large litters being born, with as many as twelve puppies, and not all of them can survive, because they just can't in that kind of environment. One unsterilized pair of dogs can be responsible for more than 67,000 puppies in a five-year period. Dogs at six months old can become pregnant, so then you have puppies having puppies. As a result, there was an explosion of dogs.

By rescuing and concentrating on that site and not taking on the entirety of Puerto Rico, we were able to clear the beach. By working with the local community and educating people about spaying, neutering, and vaccines, we have definitively proven that change can be made, and it's being made on that beach. If you walk Dead Dog Beach today, you won't even see a single dog.

To date, Chrissy's team has saved more than eight thousand strays from a life of hell. The Sato Project places those they can in loving homes, while dogs that are not candidates for adoption (because they are not socialized to be around humans) are spayed and neutered to keep them from having pups that cannot survive.[4]

Chrissy Beckles found her fight. Her heart drove her to act, and she made a significant difference for the island's animals. Other activists have saved thousands of human lives as a result of their passionate commitment to a cause.

Consider the work of Mothers Against Drunk Driving (MADD). Candace Lightner founded MADD in 1980 after her thirteen-year-old daughter, Carime, was tragically killed by a drunk driver who was out on bail in California. Candace learned that Carime was one of 27,000 alcohol-related fatalities that year in the United States. As she put it, "Drunk driving was the only socially acceptable form of homicide. Everyone was the potential drunk driver. Nobody stopped to think they could be the victim."[5]

After sharing her heart-rending story in the media, strangers began contacting her to offer support. And once Americans heard the voices of the victims of drunk driving, attitudes and laws began to change. MADD chapters opened across the nation, and thanks to their unrelenting work over the following decades—reaching out, from the heart, to families across America—every state in the country raised its legal drinking age to twenty-one. By 1994, MADD was one of the most popular charities in the country. Its efforts have cut the number of drunk driving deaths in half, saving about 350,000 lives, and MADD has helped pass over a thousand laws to regulate the use of alcohol. [6]

As a spokesperson for the National Highway Traffic Safety Administration explained, the majority of MADD members "are actually victims of drunk driving crashes. They don't want other families to go through what they've gone through."[7]

This is what authentic, heartfelt outreach can achieve. Without a doubt, success on this scale takes time. But MADD's impact has been powered by the passion and lived experience of its leaders and volunteers. Their work is from the heart, and it matters.[8]

SPEAK FROM THE HEART, WITH RESPECT

Despite the unfortunate degradation of our discourse and social media, which far too often amplify voices that denigrate and dehumanize others, the truth is, most people care about fairness and decency. So it's important to remember that you're not fighting a civil war when you engage in activism. You need to be able to sit down with those who don't agree with you. That means avoiding insults, name-calling, and trolling on social media, which are all alienating and divisive. That's not what activism and advocacy are all about. When you find your fight, you need to have your message heard by people who don't already agree with it. That requires speaking to their hearts and minds, authentically and with respect. As former First Lady Michelle Obama memorably declared, "When they go low, we go high." Inflammatory attacks may attract a lot of attention on social media, but they rarely achieve positive results. By not engaging in such low tactics and, instead, speaking respectfully from your heart, you'll have a much greater potential to change minds, change behavior, and make a positive difference in the world.

When I think of rising above, I think of the incredible work of Nicole Hockley, the co-founder of Sandy Hook Promise. One of Nicole's two sons, six-year-old Dylan, was brutally murdered along with nineteen other children and six educators on December 14, 2012, at Sandy Hook Elementary School in Newtown, Connecticut. It was the deadliest mass shooting at an elementary school in U.S. history at the time and the world's fourth-deadliest mass shooting overall. Since that day, Nicole has had to deal with her own grief, as well as devastating harassment by radio talk show host Alex Jones, who claimed that the shooting of those children and teachers was a hoax.[9]

Nicole joined me on my podcast to talk about that crushing experience, to remember her son Dylan, and to discuss her work for change in the face of harassment that she's endured from Jones and others. She spoke powerfully about the unity of her community after the shooting and the generosity of so many from far and wide—including the warehouse filled with mountains of teddy bears and paintings of the twenty-six who died, the vigils and charities that were organized, and the visit by President Obama.

At first, Nicole related, she tried to engage with the conspiracy theorists and convince them of the reality of the tragedy. She was "looking for the good" in them, she recalled:

> I tried to have conversations with them, identifying myself, explaining what happened and responding to their ridiculous hypotheses. That was a big mistake. The more I engaged them, the bolder they grew with their attacks, and their vicious hate spread to new, gullible minds, who then joined in the attack. It didn't take me long to learn an important rule: Don't feed the trolls. Don't read the comments. Don't respond to emails and block all hoaxers who reach out on social media. Do not engage.

Nicole's experience and story is heartbreaking. Yet shining through it is the power of her vision and commitment to establish Sandy Hook Promise to save children by stopping gun violence before it happens. Her approach is to focus on the good and turn tragedies into moments of transformation. Nicole and two other school families mourning their loved ones launched Sandy Hook Promise just one month after the shooting. Their goal was to study the causes of gun violence to try to prevent it. "Our mission," Nicole said, "is to ensure that this tragedy doesn't continue to happen in the future. We envision a future where no child ever has to experience the devastation of a school shooting." In all the research they've done, she told me,

> It became very clear that in order to create behavioral change, there are a lot of levers you can pull: education and programs, grassroots voices, legal action, policy action, political action. The gun violence prevention movement had only ever focused really on policy, and then, soon after, politics. But no one was teaching about how to prevent it.
>
> From all the school shootings we studied—from meetings with the FBI, mental health experts, social-movement experts, academic experts, gun owners, and non-gun owners—we developed our focus. We decided we needed to teach kids how to lead this change by showing them how to recognize the signs of someone in crisis, whether that's from self-harm, harm toward others, or harm that's anywhere on the spectrum of violence.
>
> Because there are always signs. Four out of five school shooters tell someone before they commit an act of violence; seven out of ten people who die by suicide exhibit signs and signals. These are all opportunities for intervention, and that's what we're teaching.

Those interventions are supportive, not punitive. The pillar programs of Sandy Hook Promise echo its founders' belief that you need to "create behavioral change first," then have legislation in place to enforce it. So kids learn how to be more inclusive of others and how to speak to an adult if a peer's behavior should warrant it.

By appealing to people's hearts and minds, Nicole Hockley and Sandy Hook Promise have reached tens of millions. Their programs are now in fifteen thousand schools, and they have prevented more than a dozen planned school shootings and nearly two hundred acts of gun violence—saving more than five hundred young lives in the process.[10]

The quality of Nicole's activism and the work of Sandy Hook Promise exemplify my belief in people's goodness. Despite the years of hideous harassment she endured—culminating in a nearly one-billion-dollar judgment against Alex Jones [11]—Nicole said that she sees only goodness in the faces of the young people she speaks to. At Dylan's funeral, she recalled,

> My husband and I were addressing the people there.
> I started to talk about the butterfly effect, and this
> theory that a butterfly flapping its wings on one side
> of the world can create change on the other side of
> the world. And I said that "Dylan and all those that
> we lost that day were butterflies, and their energy
> is going to create change." So Dylan is our butter-
> fly, and he is that force for change. And now, when
> I have the honor to go out to schools around the

country . . . when I'm addressing assemblies with several hundred kids, I see all their shining faces and then I see those light bulbs go off over their heads as we're talking to them, and they know that they can make a difference. And then all I see are butter-flies, because it's the kids that are going to make this change happen. [12]

When you act from the heart, you set change in motion. Your personal passion will propel you and see you through the inevitable challenges, obstacles, frustrations, and disappointments that come your way. Successful activists are strong-hearted fighters who are driven to make a positive impact on the world.

Finding the fight that moves you is the first step. So, what cause is choosing you? What do you passionately believe needs to change to make the world a better place? What issue moves you to make a difference? When you inspire others with that passion—speaking respectfully from the heart and addressing the sense of fairness and goodness shared by most people—you can build a community for change, and your heartfelt words will hit their mark.

CHAPTER 2

START WITH PERSISTENCE

"The most difficult thing is the decision to act,
the rest is merely tenacity."

—AMELIA EARHART, American aviator

Persistence, above all, is essential to your fight as an activist. Change doesn't conform to our expectations of instant gratification, calculable return on investment, or reward without delay. This can make it hard to stay motivated as activists, and *really* hard to go the distance. So, figuring out how to manage expectations, shifting course when the cause demands it, and finding joy in incremental progress are all critical lessons.

It's all about finding—and keeping—your faith in the work.

LESSONS IN DETERMINATION

I've spent nearly fifty years of my life determined to make a difference. I was eleven, in 1977, when I first felt called to help make change. I was at sleepaway camp, sitting by myself on a swing set. I don't know if I was asking God or myself, but I remember wondering, "Why am I here?"

To do something meaningful for others, I decided. To help.

My great good fortune was that my impulse had reinforcement. My dad consistently modeled an ethic of service: dishing out breakfasts or selling raffle tickets at our synagogue events and always, always working—whether for himself, his family, or people in need. I also had a very close relationship with my grandmother, who lived a modest life in the blue-collar city of Malden, Massachusetts. She cooked a lot but didn't drive, so she'd make meals all the time for other elderly neighbors and then walk those meals to the recipients' homes.

I lived with her the summer I was fourteen so I could take my first job, at a butcher shop in Chelsea. If I gained even an ounce of street credibility from any part of my childhood, it's the time I spent working for that butcher. He ran a kosher shop in a working-class neighborhood—the sort of neighborhood that, in the hot summer months, had me ducking under spray from the hydrants and dodging the kids who had opened the taps. I did daily shop runs, often delivering, on foot, a half-pound of hamburger up five flights of stairs to a customer who thanked me with a piece of hard candy. Then I'd go home to my grandmother, who would put the fifteen dollars I earned daily into a sock. I loved her so much. Today I see that job as a stroke of good fortune, since it enabled me to live with my grandmother. But it was also a bit of a primer on life—and the importance of hard work and determination.

For my father, work was a key focus. He liked to work and wanted his kids to work, even at a very young age. My dad would drag my brother and sister and me to meetings that he'd schedule on Saturday afternoons, then he'd get us to weed the grounds by the parking lot of a building he managed. We'd shovel snow, rake leaves, chop wood—you name it. But I don't remember ever feeling resentment.

Maybe I'd already absorbed the message of a quote I'd stuck on my bedroom wall. It was a Calvin Coolidge quote that my dad gave me, and I'd taped it up next to my prized John Glenn–autographed bumper sticker. The quote read:

> Nothing in this world can take the place of persistence. Talent will not: nothing is more common than unsuccessful men with talent. Genius will not: unrewarded genius is almost a proverb. Education will not: the world is full of educated derelicts. Persistence and determination alone are omnipotent.[1]

I believe that, in activism, it's the ethic of persistence that brings results over time. Change rarely happens quickly. For example, it's taken me years of work with different alliances to build programs that promote the inclusion, instead of segregation, of people with disabilities in education and entertainment. Gaining industry support for authentic representation alone took at least a decade. Real change takes time, commitment, and continued effort. Please let that sink in.

I think of what Chrissy Beckles and the Sato Project went through after a devastating Category Five hurricane hit Puerto Rico in 2007. She lost not only the ten years of progress she and her organization had achieved, she also lost her home and everything that she owned. "We were set back over a decade in one day," she told me, "and we had to pick ourselves up and keep moving forward."

As a boxer, Chrissy knows that you can't win every round. The key is to keep going. "It's not a bad thing if you get hit in the ring and you're seeing birds, stars, and disco lights playing around your head," she explained. "And taking that knee is not a sign of weakness. It's actually a sign of strength to give you a beat, to give you a moment to gather yourself, listen to your team in your corner, and then get up and continue with a better plan." With unwavering determination, she and her team recovered, and the Sato Project is now stronger than ever. That's persistence.[2]

I also think about civil rights activist John Lewis, who spent sixty years working relentlessly, inch by inch, to advance equality in this country. He started in 1960 by standing up to racists through Freedom Rides and sit-ins. As chairman of the Student Nonviolent Coordinating Committee (SNCC), he helped organize the March on Washington in 1963. Two years later, he led hundreds of marchers across Edmund Pettus Bridge in Selma, Alabama, and suffered a skull fracture when state troopers attacked the demonstrators on what became known as Bloody Sunday. In the 1970s, Lewis headed the Voter Education Project, and in 1986, he was elected to Congress, where he served seventeen terms and worked tirelessly to advance the rights of Black Americans, women, workers, refugees, and others until his death in 2020.

Over those four decades, John Lewis never gave up. Activism, he recognized, is a marathon, not a sprint. "We must be persistent and consistent. Ours is not the struggle of a day, a month, or a year—it is the struggle of a lifetime," he stressed. "You must not turn back. You must not give out. You must not give in."[3]

That's a lesson I learned early, and it has served me well. Remember that Calvin Coolidge quote and take it to heart.

THE POWER OF OUTSIDER ACTIVISM

I also learned that being a persistent outsider can be a strength.

I came of age in the era of Ronald Reagan. Because of my liberal beliefs, I was all but forced to work from the outside—a place of "difference" or opposition.

Not that I was an island. I knew my mother was a Democrat, since she'd been involved in Mike Dukakis's gubernatorial campaign, but neither of my parents ever pushed me into politics. Growing up in Massachusetts, though, I was surrounded by the legacy and idealism of the Kennedy family, with their commitment to elective office and public service.

It was the early 1980s, and the Democrats were the party of the poor and disenfranchised, the workers and the unions. And while

Massachusetts was a Democratic stronghold, my immediate community was conservative and Republican. My high school had a Young Republicans club, but there was no group for Democrats. So I formed one. Times were different back then. Sure, the Young Republicans called me a "limousine liberal," but we also hung out. We engaged in a lot of debate, and we were good at it; I eventually became president of the debate team. We scaled up and went out into the world, to debate competitions (which we frequently won) and to meetings with our congressional representative. Our small cadre of Young Democrats even campaigned for political candidates. I also served as the editor of the school newspaper and wrote really long op-eds about apathy, specifically in the context of materialism and conservatism. I suspected that I had only one reader, my English teacher, but I persisted.

Reagan was so influential. Under his watch, the materialism I wrote about proliferated, eclipsing the ideals of equality and justice. One of the first television shows to highlight this trend, *Lifestyles of the Rich and Famous*, had its debut in 1984, which was also declared the "Year of the Yuppie" (first by The *New York Times* and later *Newsweek*).[4] Despite this, I was starting to figure out, through trial and error, how to push back against what I didn't believe in—how to use my voice to advocate for an idea, whether with peers I was debating or politicians I met, and how to amplify that idea through the media.

"Outsider" status wasn't something I claimed yet, at least not overtly. But I did feel it in my culture and faith, and even more so in my Democratic politics. As a teenager, I was also very aware of the political landscape in Massachusetts, which was predominantly Irish Catholic. I was learning to be an outsider and a challenger.

After high school, I opted to attend Brandeis University. With its history of social activism, it was the perfect choice. A small, historically Jewish-sponsored nonsectarian university, Brandeis has a big history of schooling radical intellectuals such as Angela Davis and Abbie Hoffman. I double majored in politics and African studies, and I became very close to an international politics professor named Ruth Morgenthau, who had previously served as foreign policy advisor to presidents John F. Kennedy, Lyndon B. Johnson, and Jimmy Carter. I loved international politics for its more radical leanings, and when Professor Morgenthau decided to run for Congress in Rhode Island, right around the time I was graduating, she asked me to run her field campaign.

It was my first paying job in politics. I moved to Rhode Island and quickly learned how very small and tight that state was compared to Massachusetts. You saw the same people everywhere. Morgenthau suffered a massive defeat—I think because people saw her as a bit of a carpetbagger, an outsider, and too patrician to warm to (although she was, on a macro level, one of the most caring people I'd ever met).[5]

So I moved back in with my parents. Had I returned to the swing set then for another deep think about my future, I know I would have leaned toward law school. But I loved politics and the marathon of political campaigning, and I soon met a candidate named Neil Harrington. His political lineage was intense. His father, Kevin Harrington, had been president of the Massachusetts State Senate, and his second cousin, Michael Harrington, was a former congress-man from the district. Neil was a decade older than me, and he'd put in a bid to run for mayor in nearby Salem, Massachusetts, famous for its historic witch trials. Neil asked me to manage his campaign, and I eagerly joined on.[6]

Although Neil was a Salem native, I was definitely considered an outsider. Neil's opponent even attacked me in an ad for having no local connections. But I was used to being an outsider, I had a tough skin, and I was proud of the work that I was doing—organizing hundreds of volunteers who spent thousands of hours calling every single voter in the city asking for their support. We then created a Get Out the Vote program for Election Day that involved printing master lists of identified supporters that we'd arrange to take to the polls. If any supporters on our lists didn't show up to vote, we would call them to offer rides to the polling station. Our whole campaign strategy was based on getting people out to vote.

But very late on the eve of the primary, because of a software error, we couldn't get the lists to print. I was a nervous wreck. I felt like I was going to upend Neil's campaign and political career because of this technical failure. I started calling the people who wrote the software, but they never answered the phone.

"I don't know what to do," I agonized to Neil. He just nodded, standing straight as a tree. Then he put a hand on my shoulder and asked me to take a little walk with him.

"If we can't print the lists," he told me, "we'll go out there with signs. Don't worry about it." We returned to the office, ready to do anything we needed the next day to make his campaign a success.

Luckily, after many attempts to get our computer system back on board, we finally got the lists to print, and we ended up winning the election. We did it. I still recall hiding in the shadows like a wall-flower and my father's tears when Neil mentioned my name in his victory speech. It was incredible.

I was just twenty-three years old. I was an idealist, an innocent, and an outsider. I knew that I wanted to be in politics and public service, yet I hadn't come from political lineage and my political involvements were not in my own communities. But I was learning not to give up, even when things seemed difficult.

KEEP FIGHTING FORWARD

Years later, I had the honor of talking with Gloria Feldt, former president and CEO of Planned Parenthood of America. She knows a lot about persistence. Gloria is now in her eighties, but she is still as passionate and active as ever, a bestselling author and cofounder and president of Take the Lead, which promotes female power and leadership.

Raised by Jewish immigrants in rural Texas, Feldt became a teen-age mom when she was sixteen and had three children by the time she was twenty. Then, four months after her youngest was born, she enrolled in community college. "It took me twelve years to finish," she told me, but it launched her on a new path as a volunteer with Head Start, civil rights organizations, and groups that help people out of poverty.

"I relate to the hardships of young parents," she explained, "and I learned a couple of things from the Civil Rights Movement. One was that people working together can change anything, and you don't have to have formal power to do that. You don't have to have a lot of money to do that. But you have to be willing to take risks and have the courage to talk about it. And you have to work together." Gloria also realized that women were doing all the frontline work while men were getting all the leadership positions and credit. She realized at the time that women also needed civil rights to be full and equal citizens, but they couldn't unless they could make their own sexual and childbearing decisions.

She had planned on being a high school social studies teacher after receiving her degree, but she was soon offered a position as executive director of a small, fledgling Planned Parenthood affiliate in West Texas. "I thought it sounded kind of interesting and that I'd do it for a few years," she recalled. Thirty years later, she retired as the organization's national president.

She was driven, she explained, "by a passion that my daughters and all future generations of women should have the information, aspiration, and access to birth control and abortion services that give them the ability to determine the course of their own lives." She rose to national leadership after twenty-two years of experience on the front lines, serving the needs of women and families. Those experiences, plus her personal story, gave Feldt a unique perspective about the job and the importance of leading a nationwide reproductive rights movement. In her time as president, she grew Planned Parenthood's political arm into the largest and most powerful in the movement. She also led the effort to win insurance coverage for contraception and changed Planned Parenthood's stance from reactive to proactive.

Along the way, Feldt admits, she faced death threats, stalking, shunning, and harassment. But every day, she added, someone would say to her, "You saved my life." "I know what they mean," she reflected, "and that reward far exceeds any of the difficulties."

In the wake of the Supreme Court's 2022 *Dobbs* decision overturning *Roe v. Wade*, "I could despair," Gloria said, "but I don't believe despair gets you very far. We made a lot of advances, but as soon as you don't have a forward-looking agenda, you get pushed back. And that's what happened," she said, "over and over again.

"You can never, ever think that you have won. You always need to be insurgent. By that, I mean you always need to have a vibrant, forward-looking agenda—always fighting forward instead of fighting back." You must persist.[7]

DON'T RETREAT

I've been inspired by the courageous fight that U.S. Army Captain Le Roy Torres waged to win health care benefits for veterans who had been exposed to toxic emissions. On U.S. military bases in Iraq, open-air burn pits—large, open areas, sometimes the size of multiple football fields—were seen as an efficient way for the Army to get rid of all its trash, from plastics to electronics and medical waste. But the pits pumped tons of toxins into the air that found their way into the lungs of thousands of service members, including Le Roy Torres.

In 2006, when Torres was deployed to Balad, Iraq, one of the first things he noticed, he told me when I interviewed him for my podcast, *All About Change,* was the stench in the air. That was Le Roy's first encounter with a burn pit, where every form of trash is dumped and set on fire with jet fuel. The blaze, run by contractors, burned 24/7, all day and night.

Soon after he got to Iraq, Torres began having health issues that would follow him home long after his deployment. At first, he told me,

> I had a horrible cough and a bad cold. I remember going to the urgent care, and they said, "You have a bad upper respiratory infection. Your body's just adjusting to the Iraqi crud." So they gave me antibiotics and quarantined me for seventy-two hours. I was also having really bad abdominal pain at the same time, but they said, "Don't worry about it."
>
> Sometimes guys in my unit would comment on the stench from the fires, but we were always told, "It's being handled by the contractor." We trusted that what they were doing was okay and that eventually our health issues would pass—we'd go back home, and things would resolve eventually.

But they didn't. Toward the end of his deployment, Torres said, "I remember waking up with headaches. I thought, 'It's just something I'll deal with. I'll take medication.' But once I got home from deployment, my headaches and cough just got worse." In fact, about three weeks after he got home, Torres ended up in the emergency room with horrible respiratory issues. "The doctor asked me if I had been exposed to any chemicals, and when I mentioned the burn pits in Iraq, he said my body would eventually return to normal from whatever I had been exposed to," Torres recalled. "He gave me medication, but my red flags went up that day. I started realizing that my health issues were the result of the burn pits."

Torres, however, was unable to get medical help from the Veterans Administration (VA). At the time, veterans had to prove that their breathing problems and cancers were caused by the toxic smoke they were exposed to overseas—an almost insurmountable challenge. As a result, the agency denied nearly 80 percent of all veterans who requested help.[8]

"It was very disheartening for that burden of proof to be on the veteran," Torres said, "especially because I was then serving as a reservist. At Brooke Army Medical Center, they were doing research on soldiers returning home with toxic exposure issues, but I didn't qualify for it because I wasn't an active-duty soldier."

Instead, Torres was working as a Texas state trooper at the time. But eventually, he was unable to perform all his duties because of his health problems—fibrosis of the lungs, constrictive bronchiolitis, and toxic encephalopathy. Although Torres asked to be reassigned, the Texas Department of Public Safety denied his request. They also told him he would have to resign if he wanted to apply for medical retirement. So Torres resigned as they advised, but the department then refused his medical retirement application. He then went on to sue the agency, but he was so worried, discouraged, and depressed that he attempted suicide.

His wife, Rosie, however, was determined to fight for her husband and thousands of other affected veterans. So she and Torres started an advocacy group called Burn Pits 360.

"It started on our kitchen table," Torres explained, "knowing that so many others had also been affected and would be affected in the future. The challenges that I faced as a reservist with the VA and then a state employer lit this fire within us to not give up and to keep fighting."

So the husband and wife team went to Washington and lobbied on Capitol Hill, handing out printed information they had gathered about burn pit exposure. They had no luck getting legislators' attention—but that all changed when Rosie learned that comedian and talk show host Jon Stewart had teamed up with an advocate for 9/11 survivors to win health compensation benefits for them. Since the toxic emissions from burn pits were similar to the smoke, dust, and chemicals that first responders inhaled on 9/11, they won Jon Stewart's support for their congressional outreach.

After years of struggle, they finally succeeded. In 2022, the House of Representatives passed the bipartisan PACT Act to provide VA benefits for service members experiencing health issues from toxic exposure. And in June that same year, the Supreme Court ruled in Torres's favor in his lawsuit against the Texas Department of Public Safety. Two months later, Le Roy and Rosie stood next to President Joe Biden as he signed the PACT Act into law. Biden's own son Beau

Biden had died from brain cancer after being exposed to burn pits on his tour of duty.[9]

That day, Torres recounted,

> I saw the commander-in-chief as a father who had lost a loved one to toxic exposure. Knowing the effort that led us to that day was beyond imaginable. For thirteen years, we had pushed this issue, and it finally came to fruition despite the challenges that we've faced.

Torres, who uses a ventilator, will continue to struggle with health problems. But he has won his battle for benefits and compensation for thousands of his fellow veterans. When a fellow soldier was dying from toxic exposure, he remembers, he said to Torres, "Sir, don't give up on this fight. You are going to be our voice when we are no longer here."

Le Roy Torres never did give up. Despite the terrible obstacles and suffering he faced, he persevered, his efforts mattered, and he made change that will help so many others.[10]

As the Roman poet Ovid put it, "Dripping water hollows out stone, not through force but through persistence." You will have challenges, you will have setbacks, you will have disappointments. But you have to persist and keep at it. You have to find your fight, as Chrissy Beckles, John Lewis, Gloria Feldt, and Le Roy Torres did, and keep fighting forward. You cannot retreat and you cannot give up, ever.

CHAPTER 3

KNOW YOUR FACTS

"Knowledge is the antidote to fear."
—RALPH WALDO EMERSON, American essayist

When I was just starting out in advocacy, a friend and I had a conversation that I'll never forget. My friend's name was Alan Gill, and he was a seasoned activist with an international humanitarian organization. I asked him how he thought I could best have an impact on the issues that were important to me, and he offered the following advice: "If you really want to make a difference, go narrow and deep. Find a particular angle or area of focus, then narrow your scope, because when people get involved in too broad a range of issues, they're ineffective. Go narrow and deep," he repeated. "Focus on one issue, and dive into it deeply."

Without a doubt, there are infinite issues that need fixing in this world. But to be a successful activist, you need to choose your battle and become an expert on the issue that's most important to you. The truth is, activists today are competing for attention with thousands of other worthy causes. Between online and mail solicitations, the news, and social media, people are inundated with outreach for a multitude of causes, and they're all important and worthwhile. How can you stand out and make a persuasive case amid all this?

GO DEEP

To begin with, you have to speak with authority. The veracity, tone, and substance of your words matter when you're publicly advocating for a cause. When you go out with a position that's supported by deep, substantive research, you set yourself and your message apart from the slogans, memes, and buzzwords that may get people's attention but may not persuade them to act.

After the Harrington campaign, I went to law school, and it was there that I learned how to go deep. I didn't love law school at first, but it taught me how to synthesize facts and build a cohesive argument—how to separate the significant from the insignificant and how to organize and present an argument. I knew my path was taking me toward public service in law, so I dove into constitutional law and criminal procedure. I ended up working in the district attorney's office in the part of Massachusetts where I grew up. In the courtroom, I learned that speed is important. Much of a trial happens in the moment, so you have to watch, listen, and be incredibly quick on your feet. But you also have to be prepared. You have to study, plan, and know the facts of your case. Then you can argue and persuade. You have to know the law, but you also need to master the facts. Even today, before I spend an hour interviewing someone for my podcast, I spend a substantial amount of time reading and learning about them.

Even when you post on social media, you've got to know what you're talking about. Sure, speed is important. In today's media landscape, there is a huge emphasis on speed and brevity. But you'll hit a limit with memes and tweets when you're trying to make change in the world. They are too short a form to say anything of substance. Now, to be clear, I'm on social media. It's a great "call and response" tool for engaging followers about an issue, for spreading the word about an upcoming direct action, or for getting out an urgent statement as quickly as possible to as many followers as possible. But if your message isn't supported by facts—if it doesn't have substance—it won't resonate with people. It will only get lost in the thousands of other social media posts that they engage with every day.

By contrast, over the years, I've built a knowledge base that supports me when I speak out and increases the likelihood that the information will be picked up and pushed out by the many journalists and news outlets with whom I've built relationships. My reach is multiplied when that knowledge is shared, and it has much more impact than a meme or slogan.

For example, it took going deep—really getting to know the issue of disability rights, as well as the landscape of advocacy around it—to get to a place where I could strategize about the issue effectively. For me, taking a position as an activist has usually involved the commissioning of white papers, surveying, and general information gathering, then using that body of evidence to write everything from the op-eds I publish regularly to the posts I push out frequently. Over the years, our foundation has published dozens of white papers on a wide range of subjects related to our primary issues of focus. Naturally, we've also worked very hard to assemble and connect with the right people, strike at the right time, challenge in the right way, and keep our message alive in the press and social media channels. But at the end of the day, it's always the substance of the issue—the substance of our white papers—that has made us successful.

For example, in 2016 we authored the "Ruderman White Paper on the Employment of Actors with Disabilities," the first of four white papers the foundation published about the entertainment industry.[1] Our deep research found that about 20 percent of Americans had a disability of some kind. (That number now stands at 26 percent.)[2] Only 1 percent of characters on TV, however, had a disability. Of those characters, 95 percent were played by able-bodied actors with no disability. We pushed that research out to the media, and it attracted a lot of attention. We went on to publish an analysis titled "Disability Inclusion in Movies and Television," based on a survey the foundation conducted with approximately 1,300 consumers of movies and TV age sixteen and up. Of the people we surveyed, 66 percent self-identified as disabled. Our report revealed that more than 50 percent of U.S. households were likely to watch a show if it included a character with a disability. And more than 80 percent of all consumers surveyed were in favor of actors with disabilities portraying non-disabled characters.

The respondents who supported authentic representation of disability on screen tended to be younger and more technologically aware—the type of consumer who typically spends more on entertainment services and products than those in other demographic groups. Some of our research also quantified the purchasing power of people with disabilities in certain metropolitan areas. All of that advanced our case for equity and inclusion.

Thanks to our deep research and compelling arguments, ViacomCBS committed to opening all auditions to people with disabilities, and NBCUniversal, Paramount Pictures, and eventually Sony Pictures all followed suit.[3] This is how going deep can propel your activism, and it's an approach that has and will continue to achieve real results.

NARROW YOUR FOCUS

Our foundation has done deep dives on other issues, too, such as the treatment of children with non-apparent disabilities like dyslexia or various forms of mental illnesses, since these students tend to get kicked out of school and, worst case, incarcerated in disproportionately high numbers.[4] We've also researched the negative impacts of social media and cyberbullying on children with disabilities, since they're almost twice as likely to be bullied online, and the overall link between cyberbullying and depression.[5]

Several years ago, our foundation launched an initiative to move the needle on destigmatizing mental health problems, narrowing our focus within the huge issue of mental illness. The American Psychiatric Association (APA) calls the stigma of mental illness universal, since there exists "no country, society or culture where people with mental illness have the same societal value as people without mental illness."[6]

One of our narrow goals was to identify gaps in mental health resources and programs within the high school and higher education communities and advocate for policy-level changes with key stakeholders. A foundation is not allowed to lobby for legislation, but we put our white papers out into the world, and they're being used to move things forward. If our findings speak to people, these white papers will be read, picked up by the media, and used by those in positions of authority to inform policy and legislation. Our foundation's research, for example, showed that when adolescents experience symptoms of mental illness, it takes them an average of eight to ten years to access treatment. That's much too long, given that suicide is the third leading cause of death for young people between the ages of ten and twenty-four, and that more than a third of high school students with mental health issues drop out of school.[7] We wanted to make it easier for adolescents to recognize and talk about their experiences and seek help. We also wanted to dismantle the stigma that prevented them from talking about it in the first place.

Our foundation's body of research on mental health is now substantial. It runs the gamut from studies of how mental health is perceived and dealt with in Ivy League colleges to how stigma and mental illness affect first responders, including police officers, firefighters, and EMTs. We've been focusing on narrow issues within a large topic.

Take the Ivy League. Mental health issues have become increasingly pervasive on college campuses. In fact, by 2018, the American College Health Association found that 40 percent of undergraduates felt so depressed that they struggled to perform the most perfunctory tasks.[8] Many of those students were afraid to come forward for fear of repercussions. And even if they did come forward, college resources to support them were woefully inadequate. One might assume that the most elite schools in America were throwing a sizeable portion of their extensive endowments and dedicating many of the resources they have at their disposal to address the issue. Yet what we found when we went narrow and deep was just the opposite.

So we pushed out a report titled "Ivy League Schools Fail Students with Mental Illness."[9] We then raised the temperature by giving each university a grade on their mental health leave-of-absence policy. Of the eight universities we studied, none scored higher than a D+. Finally, we called for leadership and changes in school policies to reflect a deeper institutional commitment to mental health.

After our report's release, the U.S. Department of Justice (DOJ) launched an investigation into Brown University and reached a settlement with the school after finding that, between fall 2012 and spring 2017, the university had wrongly denied readmission to students who were on mental health medical leave. The DOJ found that Brown had violated Title III of the Americans with Disabilities Act, which prohibits "discrimination by places of public accommodation against individuals on the basis of disability." Brown had to pay $684,000 in compensation to affected students, make "reasonable modifications" to increase accessibility, and revise its leave-taking policies. That's a clear confirmation of the impact of going deep as an activist. We highlighted an issue and put the information out there, and it took on a life of its own. I can't draw a direct line between what we did and what happened at Brown—the DOJ may or may not have been aware of our white paper—but our report gave data to the students who were approaching the university. And by focusing on the Ivy League, we were able to get the attention of the academic world and challenge other universities to do better.[10]

SHINING LIGHT ON AN ISSUE

We also produced a "White Paper on Mental Health and Suicide of First Responders," which described the shame and stigma surrounding mental health within these professions that prioritize bravery and toughness.[11] First responders are active on the front lines of multiple emergencies, including scenes of gun violence, wildfires, and floods, as well as sickness and death during the COVID-19 pandemic. Since no one ever becomes inured to this work, it exerts a toll on first responders' mental health. I believe it's our collective obligation to support them in every way possible, so my first goal was to provoke a dialogue about the changes that were necessary for those experiencing mental health struggles to feel welcome and able to access care. I also wanted the paper to serve as a critical call to action to influential members of local communities in a position to help.

Our research revealed that police and firefighters are more likely to die by suicide than in the line of duty. In 2017, at least 103 firefighters and 140 police officers died by suicide, compared to 93 firefighters and 129 police officers who died responding to calls. The public remains largely unaware of these issues since the vast majority of first responder suicides aren't covered by mainstream media and 60 percent of firefighter suicides aren't even reported. That's shocking, and it speaks to the culture of stigma and avoidance in their community.

It wasn't a stretch to conclude that these suicides were a result of mental illness, including depression and PTSD from near-constant exposure to death and violence. We examined this exposure and reported on it, too. One study we referenced found that, on average, police officers witness 188 "critical incidents" during their careers— an outsized exposure to trauma that can lead to several forms of mental illness. PTSD and depression rates among firefighters and police officers, for example, are five times higher than rates within the general population, causing these first responders to die by suicide in considerably higher numbers. Even when suicide isn't the result, untreated mental illness can lead to poor physical health and impaired decision-making.

The antidote, in this case, is raising awareness and dismantling the stigma that still exists around mental illness in the first-responder culture of stoicism. Forcing a substantive and open conversation—within and outside the first responder communities—can mean the difference between hope and hopelessness. And by sharing our deep research on this issue, our foundation also hoped to inspire others to take up the issue in government and the broader community to provide supportive resources.

That's exactly what happened. It was probably the most impactful research we published. Material from our white paper was used as part of the background document introducing the Helping Emergency Responders Overcome (HERO) Act, a bipartisan U.S. Senate bill, in 2021. Reintroduced in 2023, the legislation was crafted to "support efforts by the Department of Health and Human Services to collect data on first responder suicides and develop and compile best practices for identifying and treating post-traumatic stress and combating suicide among firefighters and other first responders." Although we had no connection to the bill, we put the information out there. The community—local, state, and federal—realized there was a documented issue and took a key step to put mental health resources in place to help deal with it.[12]

This is the level of depth and impact I aim for with every issue I take on. But it's important to add that going deep is about more than commissioning outside research. A white paper could be a thesis or article written by anyone. If the facts you present resonate as a public issue, they can be very meaningful.

I could go on, but the point is this: with the persuasive power of research and the support of objective facts, you can achieve change. You might not be successful on the first or second pass, but you might be laying the groundwork for change in the future.

BUILD YOUR CASE

I've learned over the years that there are four steps to building a solid, persuasive, supportable case for any cause you're fighting for—and you don't need to be able to hire researchers and publish white papers to do it.

First, I'd urge you to take a 360-degree look at your issue and analyze it through the lenses of history, society, culture, economics, and politics. How have people thought about this issue in the past? How do people see it today? What are the various constituencies and positions? How is your issue represented in culture and the media? And what are its economic and political ramifications? Don't settle for a superficial understanding. Delve into the deep history of your issue, even though it may be quite complex. Understanding all these different angles will give you better insight into your cause and inspire creative strategies for how to hone your message and advance it across platforms.

Read books, research online, and keep up with the news, however you get it, especially updates about your issue. Develop a deep and current base of knowledge so you can talk persuasively about it.

Second, you need to understand the advocacy landscape around your issue—who else is working on it and how they're going about it. Activism is not a competition but it's important to know who else is focused on your issue. Sometimes you can team up with them, form an alliance, and build networks that benefit your community. Other times, that's just not possible. But knowing the landscape will help you find your niche and spot a vacuum in leadership that you can fill.

Third, you should look for every possible unique opportunity to use the media to inform and enlighten the public. That means studying which outlets, reporters, and influencers have paid special attention to your cause or have publicly acknowledged it. It's an ongoing process, because the media is fluid and the people in it change their roles and focus all the time. But it's important to identify individuals who have a personal connection to your issue, because they're the ones who can help you make your case to the public.

Fourth, do everything you can to build relationships with those media figures. This step often takes a while. You may have to meet or talk with someone several times. But once they know you and trust your research, they are likely to cover you.

When we were pushing for change in the entertainment industry, for example, we got to know reporters from *Variety*, the *Hollywood Reporter*, and *Deadline* very well. Because we developed relationships with them, we knew that we could bring them our research and have a good chance of them sharing it. So be sure to contact people who report on your issue, introduce yourself, give them timely and trustworthy press releases, and follow up with them. That is how you become a source. Then keep giving them good material, so they can share those stories with the public.

FACTS ARE THE FOUNDATION OF ACTIVISM

Academy Award-winning actor Geena Davis has successfully used deep research to dramatically advance her cause—increasing the percentage of female characters and reducing gender stereotyping in film and television. Geena, whom I'm proud to call a friend, is an advocate, archer, and one of Hollywood's most respected actors, appearing in several roles that have become landmarks and symbols of feminism, self-agency, and empowerment, including Dottie Hinson in *A League of Their Own* and Thelma in *Thelma and Louise*. Geena wasn't always as confident and loud about her beliefs as she is today, but after achieving fame and success in Hollywood, she went on to found and chair her own nonprofit, the Geena Davis Institute on Gender in Media. Its data-driven research, education, and advocacy empower and inspire content creators to reflect the diverse world we live in.

"My technique," Davis told me, "is to go directly to the people I want to influence and share data with them to encourage them to change." For example, her study of the most popular films and television shows from 2007 to 2017 found that if a woman was in the film, the character was almost always the girlfriend, wife, or daughter of the lead character. Every other supporting character was male by default, and only 5 percent of characters were women over fifty. "But there are lots of parts that can be played by women over fifty, a person of color, or someone with a disability or large body type," Davis noted.

By presenting her research to film and television creators, she's made a difference. In 2019 and 2020, her institute achieved gender parity for female lead characters in the top 100 highest-grossing family films and the top Nielsen-rated children's television programs.

Despite Davis focusing her advocacy outreach on studios and content creators, her institute's studies have found a much wider audience. They have regularly been cited in major media outlets, including the *New York Times*, *Newsweek*, *FOX News*, *Good Morning America*, the *Washington Post*, *USA Today*, the *Hollywood Reporter*, and *Variety*—ultimately reaching more than a billion people.[13]

Another great example of the power of information is NBA player Kevin Love. A five-time All-Star, Love has become one of today's leading figures in mental health advocacy. Panic attacks, he admitted, have been a constant for him since his early teens, and in 2017, he had one right in the middle of a game, in front of tens of thousands of fans. Months later, Love wrote an essay in The *Players' Tribune* detailing the shocking and debilitating experience.

After he shared his story on a national level, he realized that there was a huge community of people who were dealing with similar issues. "I had no idea the movement it would create," he recalled. "There was never another moment in my life when I was approached by more people—fans, friends, teammates, and high-profile celebrities—who shared their own struggles that they, too, had been afraid to talk about and address. It was life-changing for me."

So Love started deeply researching the subjects of mental health and anxiety and established the Kevin Love Fund, a nonprofit that works to end the stigma around mental health and give young people the tools and support they need to thrive. His vision, he explained, "is to change the conversation, find real solutions, and create resources that make an impact" through research, education, advocacy, and grant-making. His nonprofit also endowed a Kevin

Love Fund Centennial Chair in UCLA's psychology department to enable scholars to research and advance more personalized treatments for people who live with anxiety and depression.

The investment in research, he insisted, is fundamental. "If you can't measure it," Love believes, "you can't change it." Of course, you can't measure everything. But you can present the facts of an issue and say, "We have to do better." That's how you raise an issue and build momentum and a community for change.[14]

FILL YOUR KNOWLEDGE GAPS

Geena Davis's and Kevin Love's impressive impacts have both been based on deep research and data gathering. Clearly, that's a lot of work, and they funded groups and experts to do it all. But you don't need your own organization or a lot of funding to go deep on an issue that you care about. Many activists build networks of individuals to help them accomplish that task. The key—something I had to learn myself—is to identify gaps in your own capabilities and resources and enlist partners or like-minded collaborators who can fill them and multiply your own efforts.

That's what ocean advocate Emily Penn has been doing on a global scale, inspiring teams of volunteers to investigate ocean pollution. Her own activism began after she finished her university degree in architecture and traveled by boat from Shanghai, China, to Melbourne, Australia, where she had a job lined up. "One morning," she told me when I interviewed her for my podcast, "we were in the middle of the Pacific. It was a gorgeous temperature, so we stopped the boat and jumped in. And when I came up to the surface of the water," she said,

> I saw a toothbrush floating under the surface, as well as a cigarette lighter and a bottle top. At that point, we were eight hundred miles from the nearest point of land. You literally can't get any further away from people anywhere on the planet. The closest humans to us were actually in the Space Station orbiting above our heads. But as we crossed the Pacific, we saw plastic again and again and again.
>
> We stopped at small islands, uninhabited ones, that were shin deep with plastic as we came ashore. By the time I got to Australia, I thought, "I've got to do something about this," because this was an issue, at the time, that no one was really talking about. That's when I really started to learn more about what was going on.

Instead of launching her career in architecture, she spent six months organizing a community-led cleanup on a tiny Tongan island. She also sailed out to gyres of plastic trash in the middle of the ocean. "We built a trawl," she recalled, "and dragged a fine mesh net across the surface. That's when we realized that the ocean was full of hundreds of microplastics—pieces of plastic that are smaller than your little fingernail. They were hard to see and much harder to clean up," she recounted. "And then we realized that it was getting into the food chain. We caught fish, dissected their stomachs, and found plastic inside them. So it was no longer just about cleaning up our mess, but also about, 'What impact is this having on animal and human life?'"

Penn was clearly concerned about the plastic, but she also worried about the chemicals used in the production of plastic, including phthalates, which make plastic flexible; flame retardants that keep it from combusting; and fluorinated compounds, which make things water repellant. "All of these chemicals are very useful," she said, "but they are persistent chemicals—and many have actually been banned by the United Nations, because they are toxic to humans and wildlife. They're either carcinogens or endocrine disruptors—chemicals that disrupt our hormone system."

So Penn decided to investigate their effects by testing her own blood to see if any of those chemicals were in her own body. "We tested for thirty-five chemicals that the UN had banned because of their toxicity," she explained, "and we discovered that twenty-nine of those chemicals were in my blood. If we were to test for all the different chemicals we're exposed to, we might find six or seven hundred toxic chemicals in our bodies. It's hard to know at what point they might trigger cancer or some kind of hormone disruption. But childbearing women can also pass these chemicals to their babies through their placentas and breast milk. And that's when I realized how much this is a female-centered issue."

Penn then started working with teams of women who volunteered to help her tackle the problem—women who leave their lives and their jobs for a few weeks to voyage with her to all parts of the globe. "They are extraordinary women, but in a way, they're also ordinary women," Penn told me.

> They are scientists, teachers, designers, storytellers, industry leaders. We've had volunteers who work for toy and plastics companies and as package design- ers. They have a whole variety of jobs, and they come out and join us and do scientific research. We collect samples that provide data that we then supply to governments and industry to create change. The women are doing science and really getting their hands dirty—counting every piece of plastic that comes up in every single sample to characterize it and work out what polymer it is. It starts to sink in how vast the problem is and how challenging it is to solve. And they take that experience back into their lives. They can spread the word and incorporate that knowledge into the job[s] they do.

People want to do something to solve the problem, Penn said, and for the women who sail with her, hands-on fact gathering is a place to start. "One of the hardest messages that I have to deliver," she added, "is that there isn't one silver bullet solution. But the good news is that there are actually hundreds of solutions. We just need to start adopting as many of them as we can."[15]

Fact finding is something that every activist can and needs to do to build a credible, persuasive platform for positive change. You don't have to do it all yourself—you can inspire others to help you gather the facts, study the issue, and build a case. Once you know the facts, you can create an effective strategy for change.

LISTEN TO LEARN

According to former Harvard president Lawrence Bacow, you can also learn how to strategize change by sitting down and listening deeply to understand other people's lived experience. I learn so much by talking with others, in person and through my podcast. Some of those conversations are very emotional because people are telling me about the real and often tragic events they've experienced. Fortunately, they have the courage to talk about them—and as an activist, those deep conversations are essential.

When I interviewed Bacow, he noted that formal investigation is important, but it's not always enough. Deeply understanding the human side of an issue is often a critical step in solving it. "We've done a lot at Harvard," he told me,

> But it's clear, as it is for every institution in our society, that we need to do more. This is just not where we want to be as a society. And it's certainly not where Harvard wants to be. This is a time in which we need to act, but we also need to listen. There are many people who are suffering right now and suffering greatly. And those of us who have not shared that lived experience need to take the time to really

listen and listen carefully and understand in a deep way what they have gone through and what they continue to experience. And then we need to look inward, both as individuals and institutions, and ask ourselves, "What can we do to respond?"[16]

As activists, we have to learn to listen—and learn by listening. That's something that Barack Obama realized long before he became president of the United States, when he was working as a community organizer in Chicago. Obama was always studious, hitting the library instead of the bars at night when he studied at Occidental, Columbia, and Harvard Law School. But after Harvard, when he was in Chicago, he developed a great talent for bringing people together and listening to them, and their stories and experiences informed his strategies as an activist. He listened so closely that he would even turn his field reports into short stories that captured the characters and experiences of the people he talked to.

One Chicago resident, Loretta Augustine-Herron, remembered spending hours with Obama at her kitchen table. "He was not in a hurry," she recalled, "and I told him what I did working with Girl Scouts and volunteering at school as a room mother and for block clubs in the neighborhood. He wanted to know what made me tick, what my goals were, and how things impacted the stability of my family."

In an essay he wrote in those years, Obama explained why he spent so much time listening:

Organizing teaches as nothing else does the beauty and strength of everyday people. Through the songs of the church and the talk on the stoops, through the hundreds of individual stories of coming up from the South and finding any job that would pay, of raising families on threadbare budgets, of losing some children to drugs and watching others earn degrees and land jobs their parents could never aspire to—it is through these stories and songs of dashed hopes and powers of endurance, of ugliness and strife, subtlety and laughter, that organizers can shape a sense of community not only for others, but for themselves.

And through these stories, he believed, activists can gather the deep knowledge of human experience they need to make a positive difference. This, too, is a way to know your facts.[17]

LEVERAGE THE POWER OF FACTS

I can't stress enough the importance of knowing your facts before you launch your campaign for change. The deeper and more persuasive your research is, the stronger your voice will be. You need to explore every aspect of your issue, from culture to politics and economics, and know who else is working to advance your cause. You need to take advantage of every chance to inform the public through the media and cultivate relationships of trust with helpful media figures.

Once you've narrowed your focus, the next most important task is to find allies who can share the work of researching and documenting your case. And, finally, listen deeply to the lived experience of people who are impacted by your issue. By gathering and sharing deep research and human insights, you will be well positioned to make your voice heard and to make change.

PART 2

SPEAK OUT, SPARK CONTROVERSY, AND GRAB ATTENTION

CHAPTER 4

FOSTER YOUR COMMUNITY

"There is nothing to make you like other human beings
so much as doing things for them."

—ZORA NEALE HURSTON, American author

The need for community is universal and reaches across every kind of activism. To succeed, you need to bring other perspectives to the fight, bring people together around a shared goal, and nurture the next generation of advocates who can carry your fight forward.

That's why I love the idea of "seeding"—inspiring others to pick up the cause you've been fighting for. When others contribute diverse ideas about social change, they keep us from becoming fossilized in our own issues, thinking, and approaches. No one formula exists for successful activism; there is no one way to achieve change. And that's why, when it comes to disability rights, I realized over time that I needed to foster a community of young activists who could go out in the world and apply their own strategies and creativity to advance our common vision.

STRENGTH IN COLLECTIVE ACTION

I knew that the work I was doing could only continue if others contributed their energy, ideas, strengths, and voices. So we created that community—LINK20—in the U.S. and Israel. It's a global movement led by a network of young activists, both with and without disabilities, who raise awareness for the right of people with disabilities to be fully included in every aspect of life. We called it LINK20 because roughly 20 percent of the population has a disability, and these activists work to link that population to the rest of society. Our foundation created programs to strengthen the leadership skills of these young activists and build a social network that advances their goals. The LINK20 advocates and alumni continually connect to network, learn, and initiate local, national, and international advocacy campaigns.

Has it worked? Indisputably. The collective strength of the LINK20 community has already pushed through powerful changes in two countries.

One of the targets our advocates took on in the U.S. was Major League Baseball (MLB). For more than a century, MLB placed players who were injured and couldn't play on something they called the "Disabled List." But the term "Disabled List" reinforced the belief that people with disabilities were unable to participate or compete in any sports.

So LINK20 members decided to change that. Led by the late activist Eli Wolff, they signed and issued a letter to MLB calling on them to change that terminology. They created an awareness video to support the letter, then contacted MLB management to follow up. The result? After a hundred years of using the old term, MLB agreed to the change and is now officially calling it the "Injured List" instead of the "Disabled List."[1]

LINK20 activists also fought to end a discriminatory policy of the U.S. Olympic Committee (USOC) that awarded Paralympic athletes just one-fifth of the medal payout of their Olympic peers. They issued and signed a letter to the USOC stating that "the medal payout policy sends a discriminating message to our Paralympic athletes and the rest of the world, that some athletes are inferior to others merely because they happen to have a disability." The LINK20 activists urged the USOC to change that policy, and they issued a press release and created a video to raise awareness of the issue on social media.

As a result of their actions, in 2018 the USOC board voted to increase the medal payouts for Paralympic athletes by as much as 400 percent. They later issued a statement announcing that they were creating parity and equity for Paralympians—an amazing achievement.[2]

Internationally, too, LINK20 activists have launched campaigns to dramatically change social and public awareness. In Israel, for example, they've made the rights of people with disabilities a visible human rights and social justice issue. As a direct result of LINK20's efforts, the Israeli Ministry of Transport committed to making intercity public transportation accessible to people with disabilities.[3] It's a victory that will improve the lives of thousands and shows how effective the power of an activist community can be.

I celebrate when LINK20's young advocates achieve these successes. They have very little to do with me, and that's the point. Our community of skilled activists helps ensure that efforts to move the needle on these issues will continue without me—on the strong, collective shoulders of a trained, inspired, and focused community.

When it comes to making social change, nobody can do it alone. You need the power of community to keep fighting forward, because that kind of work has no end in sight. One success can't possibly stand on its own. You have to keep expanding on it—and, as we've seen with civil and reproductive rights, those gains can easily be swept away. It's a constant battle, and the goals and strategies required to take on such fights have to evolve over time.

One of the best examples of the enduring power of community to make long-term change is the National Association for the Advancement of Colored People (NAACP). Founded in 1910, it's the nation's oldest and largest civil rights organization. With more than two thousand chapters across the country, it's a multiracial, multigenerational army of activists.

The NAACP's first campaigns included a thirty-year effort to eradicate lynching. Efforts by its activists managed to drastically reduce the abominable practice, although it took until 2022 for

Congress to pass federal legislation—the Emmett Till Antilynching Act—to formally ban it. The NAACP's decades-long campaign for civil rights also scored crucial victories, among them the Supreme Court's *Brown v. Board of Education* decision in 1954, which outlawed segregation in public schools, and the landmark Civil Rights Act of 1964. In the twenty-first century, NAACP activists have launched massive get-out-the-vote campaigns, motivating a million more Black Americans to cast their votes in 2000 than in 1996.[4]

The NAACP's fight for civil rights is multidimensional and never ending. Its strength is its ability to constantly enlist new supporters and bring forward the next generation. Its long, successful history shows why activism has to be much more than a one-person crusade. To persist, you need a community behind you—and, at some point, you'll need to give way to others as the fight continues.

CREATE A COMMUNITY OF HOPE

How do you measure success? In the case of reproductive freedom, it was the law of the land, then it was overturned. Success is always a moving target. But you keep fighting because it's the contribution you want to make to the world. It gives meaning to your life, whether or not you achieve any measured success. Don't get depressed by failure because you will definitely fail. Fundamentally, activism is about hope. And the reason we fight and win or lose and fight again is because we believe—and deeply hope—that our actions will create the changes that we passionately strive for. A community of peers can lift us up when we feel defeated, renewing our sense of hope and energizing thousands of others to join in our movement. If you come out with the right message at the right time, others will support you and bring their energy, ideas, and passion to the cause you're fighting for.

For example, one Australian teenager, a sixteen-year-old named Natasha Abhayawickrama, turned to activism as the antidote for the dread she and her friends felt in response to the catastrophic 2020 bushfire season in New South Wales. Natasha realized that she couldn't have an impact alone, so she organized a countrywide event called School Strike 4 Climate. Thousands of other students in more than fifty towns and cities across Australia joined her in skipping classes one Friday and gathered with climate activists to urge the government to end funding for the gas industry.

"Activism," Abhayawickrama reflected, "has given me and so many other young people hope. There is no feeling like marching on the streets with tens of thousands of my peers, all united in our demand for real action on climate change, and in our call for the government to do more to protect future generations." Their collective action helped heighten the visibility of a critical, ongoing challenge.[5]

Community forged around a compelling issue also played a hugely powerful role in protests against the Dakota Access Pipeline project in the U.S. The $3.7 billion pipeline was planned to cross four states, carrying oil produced in North Dakota to refining markets in Illinois. The Standing Rock Sioux Tribe opposed the project because it would pass through Lake Oahe in North Dakota, a sacred site and the tribe's primary source of water.

In 2016, the Standing Rock Sioux erected the Sacred Stone Spirit Camp in Cannonball, North Dakota, to house hundreds of protesters who gathered there to call for water preservation and the recognition of federal treaties with the Great Sioux Nation. Soon, thousands more joined the protest, including dozens of other Native tribes; supporters from across the U.S., Ecuador, and New Zealand; and celebrities including actors Shailene Woodley, Rosario Dawson, and Riley Keough. Thousands of U.S. veterans pledged to protect the protesters from assault and intimidation, and businesses arrived from Pennsylvania and Massachusetts to feed them. Nearly a hundred scientists signed a resolution opposing the pipeline. Supporters of the Standing Rock Sioux also took to the streets in Seattle, Chicago, Los Angeles, New York, Denver, and other cities across the country, and nineteen municipalities passed ordinances opposing the pipeline project.

Of course, even the power of community isn't always enough. A temporary shutdown of the project, ordered in July 2020, was overturned, and the pipeline continued to operate during its environmental review. A draft review was issued in September 2023, but as of this book's writing, the fight isn't over. Two hundred thousand people submitted comments on the report, and the power and persistence of community may still prevail. As one protester put it in an October 2023 *Truthout* article, the tribes, especially the youth, are "never, never losing hope that we're going to defeat this, and we're going to protect the land and water."[6]

Community has also been a powerful driver in our efforts to bring about inclusion for people with disabilities. For several years, we organized an international inclusion summit that brought together more than a thousand global leaders in a wide range of sectors—technology, policy, human services, fashion, performing arts, education, social justice, business, housing, advocacy, sports, and more—to network, share best practices, and move the conversation forward on key issues pertaining to disability inclusion. The summit urged the disability community, which tends to be fractioned into different silos of specific disabilities, to unite to increase its social and political power. By bringing together people from around the world who care about this issue, I wanted to provide a forum for people to make their own connections, build their own initiatives, nurture the disability community, and fuel hope for continued change—the essential motivator of successful activism.

THE HEALING POWER OF COMMUNITY

Disability rights has been the issue I've focused on, but the power of community to strengthen and heal is universal. For Jas Boothe, a single mother in New Orleans who served in the military, survived cancer, and lost everything in Hurricane Katrina, nurturing and serving the community of homeless women veterans is a personal mission. Few people realize that women veterans are two to three times more likely to be homeless than any other group in the U.S. adult population.[7] That is shocking to me. People who have served our country, who have given their time and possibly been injured—either physically or psychologically—are facing homeless-ness at a rate two to three times that of any other population.[8]

"It's our duty in return to support them when their service ends," Boothe noted when I interviewed her for my podcast. But too often, long after the parades and celebrations have died down, these brave women are forgotten. After their discharge from the service, they often find themselves without meaningful support—unable to attain even the most basic levels of assistance offered to their male counterparts.

Boothe was once in this situation herself. In 2005, as a U.S. Army major, Boothe was serving in the Army Reserves as a human resources officer and was busy preparing herself and her troops for deployment. For many of the soldiers, this would be their first. She recounts,

> I was actually very excited to go into this deployment because I was a young female officer going to lead troops into a combat zone. As scary as that sounds, I was excited because leadership positions are very far and few for women in the military, especially in a combat zone, so I was excited that I had this opportunity. I was a single mom, but I raised my right hand in service like everyone else, and I took it very seriously. So I was leading all these young men and women—I wasn't much older than most of them, but I was responsible for them in every way, shape, and form. And their family members were all pulling me to the side and saying, "Please bring my son or daughter back safe. Please bring my mom

or dad back safe." It just really hit me, the level of responsibility that I had.

It was a critical year in Boothe's life for other reasons. In August 2005, Hurricane Katrina, one of the deadliest storms on record, slammed into New Orleans, her hometown. "We were at a training event," she recalled, "and a commander told us that a hurricane had hit New Orleans. People from that area usually don't evacuate—they just kind of hunker down, because storm systems come through so very often." But this was Katrina. She explained,

> My son and I lost everything we owned. Luckily, he was with my aunt in Missouri, so at least I knew that he was safe, but a lot of my troops were unable to reach their friends and family members. So we had a two-week pause, so they could find out if their families were safe. Because I had nothing left to salvage, and I knew my son was safe, I thought it would be a good time to get a medical checkup.

As if losing everything wasn't enough, Boothe learned during that routine checkup that she had a very aggressive neck and throat cancer. "It was horrible," she recounted. "I spent six months in the hospital, with two surgeries and thirty cycles of radiation." But the experience of other soldiers, she said, gave her strength and perspective going through that treatment. "So many troops," she said, "were being devastated by IEDs [improvised explosive devices]. And I would see these brothers and sisters being wheeled in—burned, some with missing limbs—and I thought, 'At least I can still look in the mirror and see myself.' I sucked it up just for them because they had it way worse than I did. It was hell going through it, but I wanted to stand up tall for them."

Because Boothe had radiation so close to her brain, she developed lifelong mental health issues and cognitive decline. But cancer was probably the easiest part of what she experienced, she said, because she left the hospital homeless. "By the grace of God, my cancer went into remission . . . after six months of treatment. Due to Katrina, I didn't have a home or job to go back to."

Homeless and jobless after her medical discharge, Boothe turned to the VA for assistance. "The lady there looked at me and she said, 'Yes, you're a veteran, but you're a woman, so you need to go get on welfare and food stamps like other women who don't have fathers that support their children,'" she recalled.

> So I went from being an army officer, having housing, and having a job to getting a couple of hundred dollars a month in food stamps to basically feed my child and nothing more.
>
> Most people don't know that over 70 percent of homeless women veterans have children in their care. And before 2011, neither HUD nor the VA tracked women vets as a homeless population. The few co-ed housing programs they had housed women veterans and their children with registered male sex offenders, because they didn't

do background checks—putting them in the worst possible situation. Often, programs didn't even take women veterans with children because the VA didn't pay them for housing children.[9] Those veterans had already gone to war and been separated from their families during their service, and now they were being separated again because of funding.

Women veterans also have difficulty accessing health care. "Not all VAs have a women's clinic," she added. "You can't get mammograms or obstetric care if you're pregnant at many VAs. I raised my right hand to serve, I accepted all of the dangers, but I am not seen as equal from a support service standpoint."

So Boothe turned her own struggle into a mission to help thousands of other women veterans. In 2010, she founded Final Salute, a service organization that provides transitional housing for women like her. "Over the past eleven years," she said, "we've supported more than eight thousand women veterans and children in more than thirty states and territories, and we've provided seventeen thousand days of transitional housing."

She also created a program called SAFE, which provides emergency financial assistance to prevent homelessness, and another called Next Uniform, which offers women veterans free business clothing, accessories, shoes, makeovers, and headshots. "When I first left the military and I was looking for employment," she explained, "I realized that I didn't know how to put business clothes together, do hair and makeup, and things like that. So we put Next

Uniform together to focus on the presentation piece, because you need more than a great resume to get a job."

Women veterans are considered second-class veterans, Boothe declared. "We've been overlooked so long, even though we've been serving for over a hundred years. Now, when people ask me what I want to do twenty or thirty years down the road, I say that I don't want this problem to exist. I don't want any veteran to be homeless, because I know that there is so much more that we can do for them, collectively, as the American people."[10]

Inspired by her own struggles, Jas Boothe became an activist for women veterans all over the country, serving and strengthening a community that lacked recognition and resources. Other activists, like Kevin Hines, have also made it their life's work to pry open minds and hearts and build a community to foster healing and change.

Hines, who has bipolar-one disorder, has reached out to millions based on his experience as the survivor of a suicide attempt. He took a personal tragedy and decided to be an activist to prevent others from heading down that path. He built a community around the shared goal of preventing suicide, shared experience, and mental health.

On a late September morning in 2000, when Hines was nineteen, he boarded a bus that would take him to San Francisco's Golden Gate Bridge, the world's most popular suicide spot. He had decided that it would be the last day of his life. When I interviewed him for my podcast, here's how he described his feelings that morning:

I believed I was useless. I felt I had no value and thought I had to die. I was wrong, but I couldn't see it. And it led me to a devastating place. I was in what I termed "lethal emotional pain," and I always ask people, "What is it that you want to happen when you find yourself in excruciating physical pain? What do you want that pain to do?" And the overwhelming answer is, "Stop, go away, or end." It was on the bus that I became what suicidologists call ambivalent. I desperately wanted to live, but I believed I had to die, and those are two categorically different things. And on that bus ride I said to myself, in my head, "If one person should say, 'Hey kid, are you okay?' 'Brother, is something wrong?' 'How can I help you?' or a variation of the three, I would have told them everything and begged them to save me."

But instead, as I cried profusely, as I yelled aloud on a crowded bus about my inner pain, the only person to react to me was a man to my left who said to the man next to him, "What the hell's wrong with that kid?" with a smile on his face. Complete apathy. And this is actually very common. This is the scenario with suicide ideation or suicide attempts, where you think, "If one person says or does this, I won't die today." And that was my reaction. If one person had said, "Are you okay?" I would have told them everything and pleaded with them to save me.

But nobody did. Even after Hines arrived at the bridge and began to cross it, he was on the lookout for someone to stop him. At one point, a woman handed him her phone and asked if he would take her picture, but she continued on her way afterward and noticed nothing.

So Kevin Hines jumped.

The 245-foot drop meant almost certain death. And in that millisecond, while he was falling, he thought, "*What have I just done? I don't want to die. God, please save me.* I had instantaneous regret and 100 percent recognition that I'd just made the greatest mistake of my life, and that it was too late. And as I fell, I thought: *This is it. This is where I go.*"

When Hines hit the water, the impact shattered the lower vertebrae in his spine. Doctors said afterward that he was two millimeters away from severing his spinal cord. But even with a broken back, seventy feet underwater—as he was thinking *I'm not going to make it* and *this is where I go*—Hines began to swim to the surface, realizing that, if he did die, no one would ever know he was aware of the fatal mistake he had just made. He continued:

> I broke the surface of the water, bobbed up and down, and prayed: *God, please save me. I don't want to die. I made a mistake.* And at that moment, something began to circle beneath me. Something large and slimy and very, very alive. I'm like: You have got to be kidding me. I didn't die jumping off the Golden Gate Bridge, and now a shark is going to eat me?

But it turned out it was no shark. It was a sea lion, and it was going to keep me afloat until the Coast Guard arrived. The Coast Guard arrived; the sea lion took off.

And Kevin Hines didn't die. Instead, he became a member of what he facetiously calls "the most exclusive survivors club in the world." He also became an activist, driven by his realization that, had any stranger he encountered that day been more aware, open, and responsive to the signs that he needed help, he wouldn't have jumped in the first place. Any single friend or family member—indeed, even a total stranger or passerby—could have helped, had they recognized his distress.

Ever since, through the Bridge Rail Foundation, a suicide-prevention nonprofit that his father started, Hines has focused part of his advocacy on legislative changes that will make the bridge safer, including the installation of suicide prevention nets. The rest of his work and passion focuses on sharing his story of hope, healing, and recovery with people of all ages, with the goal of helping them survive with resilience, eradicating suicide, and encouraging community, compassionate words, and the "friendly eyes" that could have stopped him before he jumped. He has touched a community of millions with his message, and thousands of people have told him that he helped save their lives.[11]

Let's face it. Everybody knows someone who's struggling. The explosion of mental health issues we're currently experiencing represents a crisis within a crisis in society—driven by the pandemic, the climate emergency, wealth inequity, and discrimination, all battering our everyday existence.

Of course, when it comes to mental illness, community can't eradicate the hurt. But it does have the power to reduce isolation and stigma, offer hope and healing, rewrite policy, open minds and hearts, and help people endure. That's an immensely potent force that every activist should foster.

The truth is, you can't accomplish anything alone. Every step along the way, there is somebody who can help you, and you have to work with others to be successful. Anybody who's had any success of any kind has done it with the help of a community.

Of course, partnerships and people come and go, and different folks have different views on any issue. That's okay, and it's healthy. It keeps you from being stuck in your own viewpoint. You must listen to and learn from them, stay in touch, and attend to what's happening around you, because things change. Know that you're going to fail a lot and that seeding, fostering, and sustaining a community takes time, patience, and persistence. People might not be ready for your message on your schedule. But when they are, the power of community support and activism will astound you.

CHAPTER 5

COURT CONTROVERSY

"There can be no democracy without truth. There can be no truth without controversy, there can be no change without freedom. Without freedom there can be no progress."

—ANDREW YOUNG, former U.S. ambassador to the United Nations and civil rights leader

Persistence and building community are essential elements of activism. Knowing your facts and sharing them with people you're trying to influence are every bit as important. But there's another strategy that's crucial to creating the change you're seeking—and that's controversy.

The goal of my activism is to raise issues and make them more prominent. Creating controversy is often the best way to do that. Unfortunately, "controversy" seems to be a dirty word to many in the nonprofit community and elsewhere. But it shouldn't be. Controversy is actually "good trouble," as the late Congressman John Lewis put it. It's the type of trouble that's necessary, he argued, "to enact and inspire meaningful change."[1]

Examples proliferate even within my own lifetime. Consider the success of the AIDS Coalition to Unleash Power (ACT UP) during the dreadful AIDS epidemic of the 1980s. ACT UP employed highly visible and controversial tactics—storming offices of the Food and Drug Administration (FDA), the National Institutes of Health (NIH), and pharmaceutical companies, dressed in white coats stained with bloody handprints; spattering their computers with fake blood; and lying down at their building entrances in front of handmade tombstones. As a result of ACT UP's relentless disruptive actions, the FDA finally increased access to experimental drugs and sped the development of treatments for the devastating symptoms of AIDS. At a time when more than forty thousand Americans had died from HIV and many millions were afflicted around the world, ACT UP awakened the government and corporations to the crisis, forcing them to face the epidemic and respond.

Many at the time considered ACT UP's in-your-face actions to be outrageous and extreme. But its members were literally fighting for their lives, and their controversial tactics succeeded. Thanks to the group's strategy of combining controversial public actions with deep knowledge about the drug development process, ACT UP not only got attention, it also got to the table and its leaders were able to present knowledgeable proposals that led to new medical therapies and helped accelerate the discovery, in 1996, of a life-saving treatment for HIV. This is just one example of what "good trouble" can accomplish and why, over the years, I've learned not just to tolerate controversy, but to court it.[2]

With controversy, there's opportunity for change.

Look at what happened when the #MeToo movement gained momentum. The phrase was originally popularized in 2006 by activist and organizer Tarana Burke, a Black woman who had endured sexual violence. Burke realized that it would help fellow survivors to know that others understood and empathized with their experience. In 2014, she created the hashtag #MeToo and tweeted, "It made my heart swell to see women using this idea—one that we call empowerment through empathy, to not only show the world how widespread and pervasive sexual violence is, but also to let other survivors know they are not alone."[3]

Burke didn't have a large public following at the time, but in 2017—after the rape and sexual harassment scandals of celebrities including Bill Cosby, Roger Ailes, Bill O'Reilly, Harvey Weinstein, and others—the well-known actor and producer Alyssa Milano promoted the #MeToo hashtag, tweeting, "If you've been sexually harassed or assaulted write 'me too' as a reply to this tweet." Suddenly, #MeToo exploded around the world. It was "beyond a hashtag," Burke realized. Suddenly, it was "the start of a larger conversation and a movement for radical healing."[4]

Thousands of women—many of them famous—joined Tarana Burke and Alyssa Milano in tweeting #MeToo. Their stories sparked controversy and blowback by calling many powerful men to account for sexual harassment. The movement was even accused of being a "witch hunt" that targeted men and sought to ruin their lives. But the viral campaign grabbed the public's attention. The message "creates hope," Burke reflected. "It creates inspiration." Through the power of celebrity and the courage of ordinary women, it created change. As a result of the #MeToo movement, twenty-two states passed laws to increase safety in the workplace, and many companies put in place new policies and training measures to prevent sexual harassment.[5]

USE CONTROVERSY AND CELEBRITY TO YOUR ADVANTAGE

As the #MeToo movement makes clear, the combination of controversy, celebrity, and a message that resonates with people can elicit huge attention. Celebrities have a platform and visibility that's outsized. They expect to get attention, because that's their job, and the world is attracted to both controversy and celebrity culture. So when I hear about a celebrity making a misstep in dealing with a person with a disability, I jump on the opportunity to create a public controversy around it with a targeted, well-timed message that draws attention to the issue and educates the public.

One example occurred during the run-up to the 2016 U.S. presidential election, when candidate Donald Trump publicly mocked *New York Times* reporter Serge Kovaleski. The journalist has a congenital condition called arthrogryposis that affects the movement of his joints. "You ought to see this guy," Trump riffed, mocking Kovaleski's movements and facial expression after he debunked Trump's claim of seeing Muslims celebrate in New Jersey on 9/11.[6]

I was the first person to speak out very strongly against Trump's demeaning mockery—and not for political purposes. As the head of a foundation, I can neither endorse nor denounce political candidates. But what I *can* do is comment on language. So I issued this statement to the press:

> It is unacceptable for a child to mock another child's disability on the playground, never mind a presidential candidate mocking someone's disability as part of a national political discourse. Our presidential candidates should be moral examples for all Americans and not disparage people with disabilities, who make up 20 percent of the American population.

Then, in the spirit of the teaching moment I knew this to be, I extended a respectful olive branch to the candidate:

> We would like to offer Mr. Trump a series of sensitivity training sessions to help him better understand and increase awareness on advocacy towards people with disabilities. We also call on him to offer an apology to both Serge Kovaleski and the American public as a whole.
>
> As a community that encompasses 20 percent of the American population, we have been fighting

towards a more inclusive society, and it signals how far we still must come when an individual with such authority can be so misguided and naïve in his actions.

It would be an understatement to say that the message caught on. There was tremendous outrage nationwide. Trump, nonetheless, didn't respond to our offer of training. He never apologized and later claimed that he had "merely mimicked what I thought would be a flustered reporter trying to get out of a statement that he made long ago." But the vast majority of likely voters, when asked what bothered them most about Trump in a 2016 Bloomberg Politics poll, selected this episode of mockery above all other controversies.[7]

That same year, I also called out rapper 50 Cent for a video he took and posted to Instagram while he was in an airport. The rapper decided to film a young janitor who was quietly going about his job, then posted the clip along with this commentary:

> This new generation is crazy. It's crazy. Look at him. What kind of [bleep] do you think he took before coming to work today? He high [sic] as [bleep] right here in the airport. His pupils dilated and everything.[8]

The young man, Andrew Farrell, was not, in fact, high. Rather, he was a person with autism. So I quickly called the rapper out on Twitter:

50 Cent's recent taunting of Andrew Farrell, a young man with disabilities, at the Cincinnati/Northern Kentucky International Airport is reprehensible and has no place in our society. I'm sure 50 Cent would not want anyone to publicly humiliate his friends and family in the manner he humiliated this young man with disabilities who was just minding his business while doing his job.

Although I never heard back from 50 Cent personally, the rapper responded to my criticism in several ways. He offered an apology in a statement he sent to *Billboard* magazine, which was published widely:

While the incident at the airport resulted from an unfortunate misunderstanding, I am truly sorry for offending the young man. It was certainly not my intent to insult him or the disability community, which is a source of great strength in America. I have apologized personally to him and his family.[9]

50 Cent also made a hundred-thousand-dollar donation to an autism organization. Did his publicists advise him to do damage control? Maybe. But it doesn't matter, because the incident managed to increase awareness about disability.[10]

I did something similar a few years later when Kylie Jenner—who starred in the E! reality television series *Keeping Up with the*

Kardashians and whose Instagram followers number in the hundreds of millions—posted a picture to her Instagram story of herself and her then boyfriend, Travis Scott, posing by one of their cars in what appeared to be an underground parking lot. Unfortunately, a sign indicating a disability-accessible parking spot was also shown plainly behind them.

You can guess what I felt compelled to do.

"Accessible parking is meant for people with disabilities who need it," I wrote in a statement that appeared in *People* magazine and on the web-traffic giant *BuzzFeed,* among other venues. "As a role model to many, this is an opportunity for Kylie Jenner to use her celebrity status to help society understand why accessible parking is a basic right for people with disabilities to be included in daily life."[11]

Foreign media outlets covered the story in places as far-flung as Australia and Indonesia. Which is amazing, not because I needed the publicity, but because the issue of accessibility—which, at its heart, is about human rights—catapulted into the news feeds of readers across the globe.

These experiences expanded my own understanding of influence and the power of celebrities to magnify it and foster change. The takeaway? Don't be afraid to issue a public challenge to famous people. Social media makes it easy for activists to get the attention of celebrities very quickly. In fact, Instagram may be more important than traditional media these days. Celebrities will notice your challenge, and so will the media, thus advancing your goal to bring more awareness to your cause.

I began using this approach with studios and films as well as celebrities. For example, I became super critical of big-box-office movies that used able-bodied actors to play characters with disabilities, thereby discriminating against actors who have disabilities. The first film I criticized was *Me Before You*, a 2016 romantic comedy authored and adapted for the screen by bestselling novelist Jojo Moyes. It tells the story of a paralyzed man who fell in love with his caretaker and decided to end his own life so that she could "fully" live her life without him.[12]

Let the message of that movie sink in. First, you've got the premise that death is better than life in a wheelchair. Secondly, the character who becomes paralyzed from the neck down after being hit by a motorbike was played by able-bodied actor Sam Claflin—a stunning example of Hollywood's exclusion of actors with disabilities. I was furious and said so in a public statement:

> The upcoming release of the movie *Me Before You* presents a deeply troubling message to our society about people with disabilities. To the millions of people with significant disabilities currently leading fulfilling, rich lives, it posits that they are better off committing suicide. . . . Furthermore, the movie is yet another example of Hollywood's exclusion of actors with disabilities, a social injustice that continues to be ignored. People with disabilities make up less than two percent of the film and television industries, and the movie's decision to cast an able-bodied man to play the role of the lead character is once again a sad

illustration of this. Film and television have an over-whelming influence as to how groups of people are perceived in society, and with that comes the respon-sibility for characters to be portrayed authentically.[13]

The statement attracted a lot of media attention, which was the goal. It was a major building block that helped us establish our reputation as an organization that was critical of the industry's representation of people with disabilities. I began to be seen as an outspoken activist who was not kidding around.

BE READY FOR BLOWBACK

After publicly criticizing the movie *Me Before You*, I looked for other opportunities to create debate and push the industry to do better. One notable film that year was an indie drama called *Blind*, directed by Michael Mailer, the son of novelist Norman Mailer. The movie starred Alec Baldwin in the role of a blind novelist who rediscovers his passion for life and writing when he embarks on an affair with the neglected wife of an indicted businessman.[14]

This was the era of Baldwin-as-Trump on *Saturday Night Live*, so I had a feeling I would get some attention for creating a contro-versy about his role. I guess part of me also knew that I might get skewered, but I did it anyway.

"Alec Baldwin in *Blind* is just the latest example of treating dis-ability as a costume," I wrote in a press release. "We no longer find it acceptable for white actors to portray black characters. Disability as a costume needs to also become universally unacceptable."[15]

My wife, Shira, asked me to wait before releasing that statement, because our kids were away at camp, and we were giddy at the prospect of having a whole week to ourselves. Besides, as religious Jews, we neither work nor spend time on our phones during Shabbat—from sundown on Friday until Saturday night—so any immediate fallout from my criticism, which we anticipated due to Baldwin's celebrity, would circulate while I was offline. But the press release couldn't wait. Like every other new movie, *Blind* was opening on a Friday. If I wanted to get my message out, I had to time the release with its opening.

"It's going to get ugly," Shira warned me. "You're a public figure. They'll do everything in their power to take you down." But I had found an opportunity and, for maximum impact, felt compelled to seize it. Still, the intensity of the blowback took me by surprise.

I opened my computer on Sunday, our second full day of vacation, to find myself the subject of a scathing editorial from the right-leaning board of the *New York Post*:

> Disability is no "costume" if the acting makes it real. Should Jamie Foxx give back his Oscar for *Ray*? Dustin Hoffman for *Rain Man*? Should a movie not get made if no top actor passes the Ruderman test? Mark this moronic identity-politics demand down with the new "cultural appropriation" taboo as threats to the very essentials of art—the power of empathy and the possibility of transcendence.[16]

The *Post* continued its statement with references to "dumb ideology," "nonsense," and "an attack on art." When I read it, I thought, *Whoa! This is the* New York Post. *This is one of the largest publications in America—and it's going after me personally and using me as an example of what's wrong with today's society.* But I didn't react emotionally, and I wasn't hurt. You can't fight organizations that buy ink by the barrel. I realized right away that this was not about me. It was about the issue.

So here's the thing—people might attack you personally, but they don't know you. Instead, they're responding to the issue you raised, and the news cycle will quickly move on to other subjects. You can't take these attacks to heart, but you need to be prepared. The more public you are, the more you will become a target.

In fact, the *Post's* editorial was just the opening salvo. Michael Mailer followed it with an op-ed in the industry publication *Deadline*, actually accusing me of being a fascist for criticizing his movie:

> This situation also speaks to the larger forces governing political correctness, which have become so poisonous as to ossify any helpful and progressive cultural discourse. If political correctness can be used as a cudgel to attack the very freedoms of expression the United States so cherishes, how can such a notion protect against the clear and present countervailing forces of brutishness that succeed in destroying advances in human rights? My father, Norman Mailer, an active voice against the fascistic tendencies present in America's oft-fragile

democracy, wrote many novels set in lands to which he had no physical or hereditary relationship. Because he was not Egyptian or German by birth, did he have no business writing about ancient Egypt and Hitler's youth? Art and political correctness rarely mix. And that's kind of the point. But when the requirement to be PC stifles freedom of expression, a line has been crossed.[17]

He had pulled the "Norman Mailer" card and even mentioned Hitler. So I picked up the phone to call *Deadline*, and it published my response in a matter of days. I titled my op-ed, "Alec Baldwin Didn't Cause the Problem, But He Can Help Solve It." Instead of going low, I pointed to a solution, or at least the path to a solution, and I invited Hollywood to take it:

> We are by no means discrediting the remarkable performances of all the able-bodied actors who won acclaim for playing people with disabilities. Their talent is unquestionable. We are, however, questioning why a fifth of our population is nearly invisible when it comes to one of our country's most influential mediums: movies and TV. No amount of calling our argument "politically correct" will change the reality of systemic discrimination against performers with disabilities in Hollywood. What will lead to change is a sustained commitment on all levels of the production process to audition more performers

with disabilities—a practice that in time leads to more hiring and greater self-representation.[18]

That dicey debate certainly increased public awareness of the struggles people with disabilities face in Hollywood. We raised the issue in the highest way we could. We got the *Post* to write about it because we targeted Baldwin, and we got the point across to the entertainment world. Then, through the back and forth of op-eds, we got audiences to understand that people with disabilities have a right to authentic portrayals.

Were there risks to courting this controversy? Absolutely. I learned from this experience to expect blowback—and, as a result, to be exceedingly careful about what I say, consider every single word, and never, ever go public without the facts. The rest comes down to internal fortitude and belief in your cause. If you're afraid of being attacked, you're in the wrong business. So stand your ground and keep trying to influence the conversation. Keep doing the right thing for the right reasons—to stay on the right side of history.

A CHALLENGE CAN START CONVERSATIONS

Although I didn't necessarily "win" the argument about *Blind*, I successfully used controversy to win support for authentic representation in the case of a 2018 NBCUniversal movie titled *Skyscraper*. It had all the makings of a Hollywood blockbuster. The film starred Dwayne Johnson, who played a former FBI agent and amputee fighting to rescue his family from a Hong Kong skyscraper taken over by terrorists. As far as star power goes, Dwayne Johnson is huge—so huge, in fact, that in both 2016 and 2019, he made *Time* magazine's "100 Most Influential People in the World" list. That probably surprises no one, since Johnson is also considered one of the greatest professional wrestlers of all time, known by his ring name: The Rock. He was one of the world's highest-earning actors, with films grossing a total of $10.5 billion. So I had to be very strategic about how I'd proceed.[19]

In the end, I decided to contact NBCUniversal with a question. Had the studio auditioned any amputees for this movie? That question was rhetorical. Johnson had obvious appeal, and this film was clearly a vehicle for the actor. *Skyscraper* was also the second of three very public collaborations between Johnson and writer-director Rawson Marshall-Thurber. So I knew that the answer to my question was going to be "no." That was part of my plan.[20]

It all unfolded as I'd hoped. First, NBCUniversal got back to me. A happy consequence of the credibility we had built as an advocacy organization and—this is important—because of the decency we displayed in our criticism. I can't stress this enough: if you want to seek controversy to incite debate, approach it responsibly. I've learned through experience to contact the studio involved or the celebrity's representative and say, "Look, I'm coming out with a statement. Shall we have a discussion?" That gives the celebrity or studio a chance to weigh in on the issue before I take the controversy public.

The reps from the studio didn't mince words: "What do you want?"

I replied that I wanted Dwayne Johnson to make a video calling for authentic representation in Hollywood. I wanted him to talk, in this video, about opening up the audition process, and I wanted him to name the Ruderman Foundation. That may sound self-serving, but I had an important goal in mind. In order to push studios to commit to a more inclusive audition process, I had to become a known entity in Hollywood and further raise my profile and clout as a serious advocate.

The result? Dwayne Johnson agreed to make the video, which went viral. In it, he called for more authentic representation in the entertainment industry. He said, "Our industry has a responsibility to tell inclusive stories . . . I certainly encourage the entire [entertainment] industry to take steps forward, audition, and cast actors with disabilities to play characters with and without disabilities. Disability is an essential piece of diversity, and our characters and actors should definitely, 100 percent, reflect this."[21]

Johnson also tweeted about the video, which exceeded the terms of our agreement, and the response was extraordinary. As a headline from *BuzzFeed* put it, "The Rock's New Movie Has Sparked a Debate about Disability Representation in Hollywood." I couldn't have been happier.[22]

Still, I definitely suffered blowback. Some segments of the disability community accused me of selling out, because they wanted to take a more hardline, critical stance. That's what we had always done. But I knew that Dwayne Johnson's star power, calling for authentic representation, would have a larger impact on the industry than hardline zealotry. My objective was to use his celebrity to propel the issue forward and spark debate, and I accomplished that.

Even better, I did it by working *with*, as opposed to *against*, the powers that be in Hollywood. Did that diminish me as an activist? Not at all. I persuaded a major star to produce a video supporting our cause. And I continued to challenge the industry by critiquing its output. I expanded our bedrock of research and ran ads highlighting our findings and calling for change in industry publications including *Variety* and the *Hollywood Reporter* and on social media. I sent the infographic out to the most progressive actors I could find on Twitter and asked them to retweet it. Not everyone responded, but some did, including actor and musician Janelle Monae, who has 1.2 million followers as of this writing, and comedian and actor Sarah Silverman, who has 12.3 million followers. That's a lot of reach.

WHEN TO PLAY YOUR CARDS AND WHEN TO FOLD

I can't emphasize enough how crucial it is to base your criticisms on facts. Without that, you're just making noise and annoying the people you hope to influence. Like the ACT UP firebrands who changed the landscape of drug research in the U.S., you have to do your homework first and became an expert on the cause you're fighting for. You have to have a goal—and a plan to get there—for controversy to be an effective tool. Timing is also critical. You need to know when to go public with criticism and when to hold back.

I learned that lesson when I incited controversy about an explosive issue in Poland.

In 2018, that country passed a law that threatened to prosecute anyone who was critical of the Polish government or people in matters relating to the Holocaust.[23] Unsurprisingly, the new law was hugely debated in Israel and upsetting to many of the country's citizens, since a significant number had relatives who were victims of or perished in the Holocaust in Poland. They saw it as a bogus law passed by a nationalist government that was trying to erase or ameliorate Polish guilt. Poland seemed to be saying, "We were invaded by Germans, and Germans perpetrated the Holocaust. We were just victims."[24]

That's problematic because scholars believe there was definitely Polish involvement—although not across the board, of course. Good actors existed alongside the bad in Poland. But per the country's new law, it was now illegal to say that Poland had even played a role.[25]

So I decided to say it. I produced a video that mocked the law and posted it on YouTube. The video featured actors chatting and exposing the ridiculousness of the law by saying something to the effect of, "It's against the law to connect Poland to the Holocaust. Okay, Poland, you can lock me up. Because I'm going to say it: Polish Holocaust." I also erected billboards with the same message on Israel's highways.

The issue sparked fire at once. It also sparked backlash. The Polish ambassador to the U.S. spoke out against me, as did the Polish foreign minister and even the Israeli ambassador in Poland. The American Jewish Committee (AJC) issued a statement decrying the video, insisting that their organization had already made its opposition to the legislation clear and accusing me of messing things up by creating controversy around an issue that was already so contentious.[26]

It was a risk, but controversy was my intention. I believed that this issue deserved to be discussed openly, by members of the public with different opinions. The idea that a group—which, in my view, isn't fully representative of that public—was "handling" things behind the scenes smacked of a "stay away" attitude toward activists.

In response, I defended our actions and did a lot of interviews. But then we were contacted by some Jewish people in Krakow, Poland, who told us that our public attacks were making things uncomfortable for them. That was never our intention. So we pulled the video, twenty-four hours after posting it. We felt it was time to defuse the public controversy we had created, because we were causing a lot of stress for people we were trying to help. But a few days later, the president of Poland personally addressed the Jewish community, so I know that we had touched a nerve in Poland.[27]

Issues are complex, and the more you know about every side before stoking controversy, the more successful your public criticism will be. You may become a target, and your actions may have unintended effects. But when you provoke controversy with the right message at the right time—leveraging the power of celebrity with respect and with the facts behind you—it can have astounding impact. By drawing public attention to your cause, you can educate the public; call people, organizations, companies, and governments to account; and accelerate change. Through my own experiences courting controversy as an activist, I discovered that the strategy really works—but it's important to know when to take a step back for the good of the cause you are fighting for.

CONTROVERSY CREATES SOCIAL PRESSURE

I have often been called a gadfly—"a person who stimulates or annoys other people, especially by persistent criticism," according to *Merriam Webster Dictionary*. The ancient Greek philosopher Socrates was known as the "gadfly of Athens" because he was always challenging the status quo with novel, deliberate, and often upsetting questions. I like to stir up controversy because it leads to social pressure. In some cases, that pressure comes from the public. In other cases, it can come from individuals who exert influence.[28]

Social pressure is crucial to achieving change. Putting information out there is never enough; behavioral research backs this up. Information can help change a person's opinion, but the social delivery of that information has much greater impact.[29]

Alcoholics Anonymous is a great example of the power of social pressure turned to good. It's all about being part of the group and staying sober by being accountable to a group as well as to your individual sponsor. Another example is social pressure to stop smoking. Peer pressure is often the reason that many young people start smoking in the first place—but quitting is much more difficult, and many smokers can't do it on their own. For decades, American culture strongly promoted the use of tobacco. So why did the percentage of American smokers drop from 45 percent in 1971 to 21 percent in 2003? It wasn't just information about smoking's dangers. Studies showed that it was social pressure. As one researcher explained, smokers used to be the life of the party, but over time they became wallflowers. Smoking became bad for their social, as well as physical, health. It turned out that people stopped smoking in groups, not individually—and those who refused to go along with their group's behavioral change became isolated.[30]

That is the power of social pressure. When you combine information with social influence and personal experience, it makes a difference. People change when an issue touches them personally—and if you apply that dynamic to the changes you seek as an activist, you'll have a stronger chance of succeeding over time.

That's been true in my own work. For example, when our foundation was invited to partner with the Israeli government and the American Jewish Joint Distribution Committee (JDC) to create a new Israeli department focused on including people with disabilities in society, I was excited. It was a great opportunity to develop new government pilot programs and policies that support inclusion, instead of segregation, of people with disabilities. For a significant portion of the population, that had the potential to change everything.

But surprisingly, although I came in as a full partner with JDC and the Israeli government, I didn't have equal voting rights. I had a seat at the table and was invited to participate in meetings, but I was offered no role in decision-making. I realized that, as an American, I was an outsider, so my influence was extremely limited. But that changed, thankfully, once I enlisted my Israeli wife, Shira, in the project. She was able to communicate our perspective in our partners' language—not just literally, but culturally and experientially, as a true Israeli. She's also smart, expressive, and acutely social. Shira was able to exert the social pressure we needed to be heard by our Israeli partners. Her presence at the table fostered trust, increased our influence, and helped make positive changes.

As a result, our partnership accomplished a great deal. We helped move Israeli policy from a segregated model to an integrated one. Our work resulted in the establishment of a new Disability Administration in the Ministry of Social Affairs, with flexible supports that respect people with disabilities as individuals. All told, our efforts have led to the creation of fifty programs, twelve government partnerships, and twenty-eight business collaborations—affecting the lives of more than 340,000 people. We've helped change the attitudes of Israelis toward people with disabilities and the way Israelis with disabilities view themselves.[31]

START A CHAIN REACTION

Even if you don't personally know people with influence, you can leverage public controversy to attract their attention and support. How do you start? It's a lot like a game of dominoes, where you tip one block, which tips the next, and so on, until they all fall.

That's what took place in San Francisco in the 1950s, when the State of California planned to construct new freeways that would run through residential neighborhoods. This would require the demolition of homes and businesses and forever change the character of the city. A few alarmed residents realized those freeways would tear up the communities they loved. One of them started publicizing the controversy by going door-to-door and sending mailings to warn neighbors about the plans. A couple of other community members spoke up at a public meeting and won the support of a parish priest and a city supervisor. With that backing, they were able to enlist neighborhood organizations in the cause. By the end of the decade, the issue became so hot that the city's Board of Supervisors voted unanimously to reject the construction plans. That successful movement was known as the San Francisco Freeway Revolt.[32]

It's an almost perfect model for how to build social pressure for change. I've seen activists be fabulously successful following the same principles on social media, and you don't need a lot of resources to do it. You don't have to send mailers or print flyers. You just need to use your creativity and talents. The Freeway Revolt happened long before the advent of social media, but its basic principles still hold—the importance and impact of person-to-person persuasion and the power of enlisting people with influence to your cause.

On an international level, that's what led to the end of apartheid—or institutionalized racial segregation—in South Africa. It took thirty-five years, but it was public controversy and sustained social pressure that led to change. It started when international sports competitions protested the practice by excluding South African athletes. As internal unrest and civil disobedience in South Africa increased, foreign banks began calling in their loans and pulling out of the country. Europeans pressured retailers to stop selling South African imports to increase economic pressure on the country. University students in Europe and the U.S. mobilized and demonstrated against apartheid, resulting in financial sanctions and divestment. It was controversy, social pressure, and shunning on a global scale. When South Africa finally ended apartheid, the decision was motivated, in large part, by a national desire to end the punishing boycotts and isolation.[33]

Social pressure, as you've seen, is a powerful tool. It may take years to build enough pressure to succeed, but it can lead to important behavioral, social, and political changes. The more influential people you persuade, the more attention you will get, and the more people in power will want to listen to you.

STARTING FROM THE TOP

Leadership is another powerful form of social pressure. It can come from the top as well as the grassroots, and both forms can be extremely impactful. I've had a number of interesting conversations about this on my podcast, *All About Change*. One of them was with journalist Judy Woodruff, whose decades of experience in broadcast media make her especially qualified to comment on how we engage with each other publicly, and how the tenor of that engagement has changed as a result of America's leaders and role models.

When we talked a few months before the 2020 U.S. presidential election, I asked her if she thought we'd ever return to a more balanced and respectful public discourse. She said:

If we have leaders who model respectful discourse and who model respectful conversation
and exchange . . . I think that could go a long way
toward affecting the American people. But without
that, I don't see how we turn it. So we have to take it
upon ourselves to say, "That's not acceptable," and
I think we do that inside our families. We try to
teach our children to have the values that we think
are the most important: values of compassion and
respect and honesty and integrity. And my hope is
that those will override some of these other more
negative values that we see being demonstrated in
public life.

Woodruff also pointed to the importance of regular people taking it upon themselves to recognize when some behavior is not
acceptable and to model respect. That is very relevant to activists—
all the more so if they're visible and vocal (as I recommend they
be) in traditional and social media. Go high when others go low, as
Michelle Obama urged. What the world needs is your moral com-
pass and positive example as an activist.[34]

Our era is not the best, nor the most balanced and respectful,
when it comes to public discourse, but that doesn't mean we can't
choose to do better. So if you're engaged in a cause publicly and
want to show leadership, consider your position on negativity. Do
we really need to rip others down? I would argue we don't. It's coun-
terproductive and the opposite of effective critique.

In her memoir, *My Life on the Road*, feminist activist Gloria Steinem described talking circles as "groups in which anyone may speak in turn, everyone must listen, and consensus is more important than time." Steinem was schooled in that mode of discourse, which she first encountered in India, where she conducted a fellowship after she graduated from Smith College in 1956. She saw how Gandhi and the women of India would use the "talking circle" as a way to start a grassroots movement, and this was where she first ignited as an activist.[35]

This approach might sound terribly old school in the context of today's noisy, instantaneous social media, but it certainly lines up with the more balanced and respectful manner to discourse that I want to encourage. No question, times have changed, but Steinem continued to exercise a version of this inclusive approach—listening to a diversity of voices—as she weathered her decades of controversy. As she put it, "I don't learn while I'm talking. I learn while I'm listening." Those of us who desire a departure from the vitriol and division of public discourse today can choose to see that as a model.[36]

So reach out and try to persuade people with influence. They can bring many others to your fight and start a chain reaction. If you persist with this strategy over time, you can heighten the energy behind your cause until it's such a hot issue that it will ignite change.

But stay on the right side of social pressure. Don't be lured into the trap of cancel culture. It's a dead end. Take the high road and be a leader who encourages dialogue, listening, civil discourse, and even praise. Through sustained social pressure, you may eventually see your cause carry the day.

CHAPTER 6

LEVERAGE POWER

"A life isn't significant except for its impact on other lives."
—JACKIE ROBINSON, first Black player
in Major League Baseball

To be an effective activist, you have to do more than yell at businesses and institutions from the outside. You have to find a way to work from the inside, too. But how do you get inside access? With the help of like-minded individuals who can get you a seat at the table. Those individuals can leverage their social power and connections to help you advance your cause. They're essential links in the chain of influence and key players who can start tipping the dominoes.

Much of my own success as an activist has been due to the involvement of a select group of exceptionally good and talented people with powerful influence in the entertainment industry.

Aligning with them greatly increased my own relevance and ability to make change. Because their interests paralleled mine, we were able to come together and work together in service of the greater good.

FIND INSIDER ALLIES

The tide began turning for me after I decided to go "narrow and deep" on disability rights. My efforts to get to know the advocacy landscape in the field forged lots of important connections. One of them was actor Danny Woodburn, who had written and published an op-ed in the *Huffington Post*. The title of his piece said it all: "If You Don't Really Mean Inclusion—Shut the F%&# Up!"[1]

Woodburn is a little person. He is four feet tall and was born with spondyloepiphyseal dysplasia congenita (SEDC). He has starred in dozens of movies and TV shows throughout his career and won the 2010 Screen Actors Guild Harold Russell Award, which recognizes an individual who has substantially contributed to the overall awareness of the disability experience through media. Woodburn is probably best known for his recurring role as Mickey Abbott, Kramer's volatile friend, on NBC's Emmy-winning sitcom *Seinfeld*.[2]

When Woodburn first went to Hollywood, he pounded the pavement for a long time. "I didn't want to be a sight gag," he explained. "I didn't want to be mocked on screen or laughed at. I wanted to be 'in' on the joke as an actor. I wanted my characters to be three-dimensional and not just there as a prop, as so many types of little people roles had been."[3] Landing the *Seinfeld* gig jump-started Woodburn's career and enabled him to give voice to his concerns once he finally "got in the room."

But he found other audition opportunities sorely lacking. So he started advocating for change from inside the industry. I know many actors with disabilities who are activists and commercially successful. But their advocacy is tempered by the fact that they have to work and don't want to be blackballed. Then there's Danny Woodburn, who has always been courageous in his activism and publicly outspoken about the need for diversity and equity in the media.

Woodburn went on to collaborate with us on several white papers. He also introduced me to the talented Farrelly brothers, Peter and Bobby. Peter Farrelly is an Academy Award and Golden Globe winner who wrote and directed the amazing 2018 film *Green Book*. Along with his brother, Bobby, he's also responsible for such memorable comedies as *Dumb and Dumber*, *Shallow Hal*, and *There's Something About Mary*. The two brothers are incredibly funny and successful, but they are also fantastic people—open, honorable, and genuine. Good people make good partnerships, and for me, Peter and Bobby are the consummate partners. And they happen to be directors who are committed to the full inclusion of people with disabilities in the entertainment industry. As Bobby put it, "Twenty percent of the population has disabilities, and if you don't have something like that in your movie, it's not a real world. We were trying to write reality. We wanted people to recognize the world they were in."[4]

A world involving people with disabilities has always been real for the Farrellys, as it is for most of us. When the brothers were young, Bobby recalled, they hung out with the other kids in the neighborhood, some of whom had what we would now call "intellectual disabilities." But, Bobby added, "They'd be part of the gang. If we were playing a game of touch football, they'd be in it."

So it didn't take much, Peter explained, to add characters with disabilities to their stories. He was also present when a friend of theirs, the late Danny Murphy, was paralyzed from the chest down after diving into shallow water. Peter and Bobby have been very up-front about how Murphy guided them in their disability rights activism:

> It was Murphy who said, after *Dumb and Dumber*, "Hey, what's going on? I didn't see a lot of disability in there." And I was like, "You're right," and that changed it right then because we were very comfortable. We had two friends who broke their necks in high school, so we had wheelchairs all around us. Everybody was in vans, going to parties.[5]

They decided to include people with disabilities in the stories they tell because they were a part of their lives, and it wasn't a real world if it didn't include everybody. But it also isn't a real world if only able-bodied characters in movies are flawed and funny, while those with disabilities are depicted as saintly, inspirational, and one-dimensional. The Farrelly brothers didn't want to glamorize characters with disabilities. Instead, they use their typical brand of mockery and humor, often at their expense. In writing about *any* community in their comedies, the Farrelly brothers are going to be funny. In fact, they have two scripts listed on the Writers Guild of America's list of "Top 100 Funniest Screenplays of All Time": *There's Something About Mary*, at number eighteen; and *Dumb and Dumber*, at number fifty-four.[6]

Peter and Bobby followed Murphy's challenge with one of their own. They insisted that he be in their next movie. So Murphy took a lot of acting classes and launched a career as a professional actor. The experiences he had in Hollywood further educated the brothers. Peter told me that

> It was almost impossible, rare, that someone in a wheelchair would even get an audition. And if Murphy did, a lot of the time, he would get to the audition but couldn't get in the building. They literally didn't have the accessibility to get him in the building and up the stairs, so they'd have to come out and audition him on the sidewalk, with people walking back and forth. It was awful. That opened our eyes.

Peter and Bobby seemed to be natural allies. Since I wasn't seeking any financial gain or position in the industry, Peter, especially, agreed to work with us to convince studios to open their auditions to actors who have disabilities. I hoped that the studios would articulate that commitment by making what I call the Ruderman Pledge:

> We recognize that disability is central to diversity, that the disability community comprises the largest

minority in our nation, and that people with disabilities face seclusion from the entertainment industry. We understand that increasing auditions, no matter the size of the role, is a critical step toward achieving inclusion in the industry. This studio pledges to increase the number of actors and actresses with disabilities who audition for parts on television and in film.[7]

I had already successfully won the support of ViacomCBS, thanks to the leadership of Tiffany Smith-Anoa'i, its Executive Vice President of Diversity, Inclusion & Communications. She had shown remarkable leadership by insisting that ViacomCBS become the first major media company to make the pledge. She saw immediately how meaningful that was on a human level and what it could yield in terms of positive media coverage. But while ViacomCBS became a very public partner, other studios were more resistant. They understood what we were asking of them, but they were hesitant to move forward. We needed someone on the inside to help us close the deal.

Enter Peter Farrelly. *Green Book* had just won the 2019 Academy Awards for Best Picture, Best Original Screenplay, and Best Supporting Actor. After he picked up the phone and called the heads of NBCUniversal, Sony, and Paramount to make the case for them to take the Ruderman Pledge, each studio, within months, issued announcements about their commitments to disability inclusion. Peter generously leveraged his power to advance our mutual cause—and that, combined with our own compelling arguments and research, moved the needle. Because Peter could, he opened doors, and for that I'll always be grateful.

That year, we honored both Peter and Bobby Farrelly with the Morton E. Ruderman Award in Inclusion for their outspoken efforts to make movies more inclusive and authentic. The award is named after my father, Mort Ruderman, who founded our family foundation and was passionate about providing opportunities for others. Peter, with characteristic humility, insisted they "didn't deserve" the award, but of course they did. And the phone started ringing almost as soon as I announced that we would honor them at the Waldorf Astoria Beverly Hills. Many celebrities attended, including Marlee Matlin, Danny Woodburn, Ted Danson, Mary Steenburgen, Larry David, Cheryl Hines, Kevin Nealon, Kevin Pollak, Ron Livingston, and former New England Patriots receiver Julian Edelman. Peter and Bobby even flew their mom in from Rhode Island. I recall gazing out at the room full of industry leaders, all buzzing with excitement, and thinking, *Wow. Not that long ago, the issue of authentic representation for people with disabilities in Hollywood barely existed on anyone's radar. Now it's front and center in this room and in the industry.* And much of that is thanks to our extraordinary allies on the inside and outside. [8]

IT'S NOT ABOUT MONEY

Let me make one thing crystal clear: you don't need wealth or connections to leverage power like that for a cause you care about. What you do need is commitment, persistence, and credibility. One of the most compelling examples I've ever encountered involves a California teenager named Genesis Butler. Butler is an environmental activist focused on animal rights. At age three, when she learned where chicken nuggets came from, she decided to stop eating meat. By age ten, after she began posting on social media about animal rights, she gained thousands of followers. And as a result of her activism on that platform, Butler became one of the youngest people to give a TEDx talk, entitled "A 10-Year-Old's Vision for Healing the Planet."[9] She has since been featured in dozens of news articles and has won many accolades, including Sir Paul McCartney's Young Veg Advocate award. Butler has delivered her message in Rome, Milan, Paris, Brazil, the UK, and at Moby's Circle V Festival. She has personally spoken with celebrities including McCartney and famed anthropologist Jane Goodall. She has even challenged the Pope to go vegan and has been featured on the Disney show *Marvel's Hero Project*, which profiles young people making a difference in their communities and the world.

When I interviewed Genesis on my podcast, I asked her how she started to win global attention as an activist. After building an animal-rights following online, she told her mom that, when she was older, she wanted to give a TED talk. "But I didn't know it would happen so soon," she told me.

I got a message asking me to apply to do a TEDx talk near me, so I did—just to see if I'd be able to get in. There were so many people applying, and I'm really young, so maybe they wouldn't pick me, I thought. But then I got chosen to give the talk, and I realized that people do want to hear my message. That helped me become more of an activist and start realizing the power of storytelling. The TEDx talk also helped me shift from being an animal-rights activist to more of an environmental activist. That has been my main focus, because I have a little sister and I want her to have a thriving planet.[10]

The power and reach of the TEDx platform opened doors for Butler. The next year, at age eleven, she founded her own nonprofit organization, Genesis for Animals. Then, during the COVID-19 pandemic, she started a global youth-led climate organization called Youth Climate Save, which now has around eighty chapters in twenty-two countries around the globe. Butler also constantly participates in protests, beach cleanups, and tree plantings. She takes every opportunity to educate people and get other youth involved. She has also successfully campaigned for legislation to offer vegan meals in nursing homes, hospitals, and prisons, and her growing profile has led to invitations to speak at climate conferences and summits. "It was very hard for me to start getting into these environmental spaces," she acknowledged, "but now I've been speaking at them."

Genesis has literally earned a seat at the table, thanks entirely to her own passion and outreach. Although the scale of the climate crisis can feel overwhelming, she says it's crucial to stay engaged and optimistic about the future. "Using my voice has always helped me," she says. "I know that at least I'm doing something about it, however I can."[11]

If someone like Genesis Butler can build her profile and credibility enough to leverage power through influential groups, events, celebrities, and media, it's within the reach of almost any activist. If your message speaks to others, you can attract insiders to help you. With persistence, passion, and creativity, you can make it happen.

INFLUENTIAL ALLIES ARE LIKE MEGAPHONES

Powerful insiders can also help you spread your message to a wider audience. That's what TEDx did for Genesis Butler, and she's continuing to leverage the reach that platform gave her. In our case, Peter Farrelly connected me with Octavia Spencer, who won the Academy Award for Best Supporting Actress for her role in *The Help* and was twice nominated afterward for her contributions to *Hidden Figures* and *The Shape of Water*. Spencer agreed to do a brilliant public service announcement for us imploring the entertainment industry to increase the casting of people with disabilities. In the video, she recalled the theatrical industry's history of inauthentic representation and exclusion of marginalized populations—from men playing women until the seventeenth century and white actors playing Black, Asian, and Native American characters to the omission of LGBTQ+ figures from film and television until the twenty-first century. As a result, their stories were portrayed and told inauthentically, she declared in the video.[12]

> But nothing can replace lived experience and authentic representation. That's why it's imperative that we cast the appropriate actor for the appropriate role, and that means people with disabilities as well. Casting able-bodied actors in roles for characters with disabilities is offensive, unjust, and deprives an entire community of people from opportunities. There is no reason that we should continue to repeat the same mistakes of the past. Together, we should and can do better.

Octavia Spencer is a superb partner. She wanted nothing in return for her work with us—only the opportunity, she told us, to "do better" together.[13]

Actor Marlee Matlin is another friend and ally who has used her fame to help amplify our message of inclusion. Matlin is well known for her advocacy in Hollywood. She is also one of only three Academy Award–winning actors who happens to have an identifiable disability. I suspect that anyone who's seen her incredible performance in the 1986 film *Children of a Lesser God*, in which she plays a deaf person in love with her speech therapist, will never forget it. In addition to her Oscar, Golden Globe, and multiple

Emmy nominations, Matlin has authored several books—among them, the novel *Deaf Child Crossing,* and her recent memoir, *I'll Scream Later.*

Matlin and I have become friends, and it was with her at my side (along with Danny Woodburn and the Farrellys) that our cause began to gain momentum. I also witnessed firsthand the power of her celebrity for good when she—along with her manager and life-long interpreter, Jack Jason—joined me on a trip to Israel, where I presented her with the Morton E. Ruderman Award in Inclusion. We held an event in Matlin's honor at the Tel Aviv Cinematheque, where she was besieged by adoring fans. That event will live forever in my memory because of all the different interpreters who were present. Since there is no universal sign language, every country or region has a distinct version. As a result, we convened with multiple interpreters working in American Sign Language (ASL), Israeli Sign Language (ISL), and the particular form of Arabic Sign Language (ArSL) used in Israel. It was really something. That afternoon in Tel Aviv, she told the crowd:

> No matter what barriers we face, I believe we all have a unique gift to share. I also believe we have an obligation to impact the world, beyond what society thinks we can and can't do, particularly on behalf of those who don't have access to the resources to realize their dreams or help themselves. It's unfortunate that for every step I've taken forward, there are still millions out there who face discrimination, misunderstanding, and rejection.

That's Marlee Matlin. She has been a constant, passionate advocate for disability rights and a champion for authentic representation. By leveraging the power of her celebrity, we have been able to reach a much wider audience with our message.

In 2021, Matlin took the stage at the 93rd Academy Awards ceremony to introduce the nominees for Best Documentary Short and Best Documentary Feature. Her presence spoke volumes about Hollywood's changing attitudes toward full inclusion—something I hoped I had some influence on. Two months later, Matlin joined fellow Academy Award winners Whoopi Goldberg, Sophia Loren, and Buffy Sainte-Marie to help inaugurate the Academy Museum of Motion Pictures with a panel event on "Breaking the Oscars Ceiling." And she took the stage again in 2022 at the 94th Academy Awards ceremony to celebrate the groundbreaking Best Picture winner, *CODA*—a film, in which she starred, about a deaf fishing family with a hearing daughter.

Over the years, I've learned to be open to what partnerships can bring. I've focused on the power of celebrity, but all relationships worth their salt yield something of value to those who are in them— even if that something is friendship or a deeper understanding of the shared cause. Individuals can be a force, especially when they're leveraging their power for the greater good.

MOVE FROM CHALLENGE TO COLLABORATION

Here's another important lesson to learn as an activist: if you're always criticizing and telling people what they're doing wrong, they will eventually stop listening and tune you out. So at some point, you'll need to shift from challenge and provocation to collaboration. You need to work with those you are challenging to change policy, then credit them when they move in the right direction.

In the beginning, controversy was a way to draw attention to myself as a disability rights activist. Being critical and controversial got me press coverage and standing. I built my platform through notoriety based on honest criticism. But courting controversy was never an end in itself. I didn't want to get stuck where so many people languish—in the churn of endless criticism. Instead, once I'd gained a lot of exposure as a gadfly, I also wanted to offer strategic incentives to those who were, or might one day become, allies.

So after ViacomCBS agreed to the Ruderman Pledge, I knew it was time to start formally acknowledging studios and individuals for the good work they were doing, instead of just criticizing them for the bad. That's why, in 2019, I introduced the Ruderman Seal of Approval for Authentic Representation. The idea was that our Seal of Approval would function as a carrot instead of a stick—a means of incentivizing people in the entertainment industry to demonstrate a commitment to full inclusion. A big advantage of the award was positive media exposure. I had already established a reputation in the media—through our white papers and challenges—as a critic in matters of authentic representation and disability rights. I'd also worked very hard to maintain my relationships with top journalists at the *Los Angeles Times*, *Deadline*, *Variety*, and the *Hollywood Reporter*. Because they knew me as a serious activist, they went on to cover the Seal of Approval and those who won it—recognition that show runners, casting directors, and actors appreciate.

We gave our first Seals of Approval to Netflix's *Special* and *The OA*; NBC's *Speechless*; and CBS's *NCIS: New Orleans*—all shows that featured actors with disabilities. The next year, our winners included the movie *The Peanut Butter Falcon*, about a man with Down syndrome. The film starred Zack Gottsagen, an actor who has Down syndrome, and co-starred Shia LaBeouf.

It was almost a miracle that *Falcon* ever got made. Directors Tyler Nilson and Michael Schwartz couldn't find funding for it because it was going to star Gottsagen. As Nilson explained, several studios offered the pair an increase in budget if they were willing to cast an A-list, able-bodied person in the lead role. But though the two were living on the edge of poverty—"I was eating just enough food, calorically, to get by; one piece of chicken, one half of sweet potato, and one spoonful of butter daily," Nilson remembered—they refused to have anyone but Gottsagen as the star. "Deep in my heart," Nilson said, "I knew that somehow, somebody would step up and say they were going to fully support this movie."[14]

Someone did. To this day, I have a hard time describing the pride I felt when I saw *The Peanut Butter Falcon*'s Zack Gottsagen take the stage at the 2020 Academy Awards to present along with his co-star Shia LeBeouf. What Gottsagen did to get there is wholly to his credit. But as an ally on the path, I couldn't have been happier.

So here's the point: after you've gathered your facts and raised your profile as an activist by courting controversy, the next step is to leverage your growing power by enlisting allies in the cause who can leverage *their* power, in turn, to help you. Those partners can get you a seat at the table or broadcast your message to a much wider and more influential audience.

Bottom line, as an activist, I'm happy to be a gadfly and issue a challenge. I can certainly wield a stick, but I'll also offer a carrot when it's more effective. What I really want to do is change people's minds. I'll work to do that through criticism, controversy, contacts, leadership, praise, and every form of social pressure and leverage that I can muster.

Once the people who can make change have heard your message, it's time to shift from challenging them to collaborating with them, helping them to do better and praising them for making positive progress. You have to give credit, because you need allies to continue. People love recognition for doing the right thing. That's how you build an alliance. And when your allies and partners pull together with you, it might be surprising how quickly you can make a difference.

PART 3

MAKE PROGRESS AND MARK YOUR PROGRESS

CHAPTER 7

TAKE CARE

"Caring for myself is not self-indulgence, it is self-preservation,
and that is an act of political warfare."

—AUDRE LORD, American writer and professor

A ctivism is a high-stress endeavor that can take a toll on your physical, mental, and emotional well-being. No matter how committed you are to your cause, the pressure of controversy and struggle can wear you down. Long-term exposure to the suffering of others can lead some activists to experience "compassion fatigue"— an overwhelming sense of despair and heartbreak.

But if you become despondent or burned out, you can't be an effective activist. If you're anxious, exhausted, cynical, or sad, you won't be able to bring the creativity, energy, and focus it takes to make a difference. That's why you owe it to yourself—and your cause—to take good care of your physical, mental, and emotional health. It's essential if you're working to make social change.

FIND YOUR BALANCE

I've learned that maintaining my well-being and health is fundamental to my ability to persist and succeed as an activist. That's why I strive to eat a healthy diet, instead of grabbing fast food on the run. I make a point of not skipping meals, and I spend an hour exercising every day. My daily gym workout of weightlifting and cardio keeps my body strong and boosts my energy and mood. Whatever I might be dealing with—no matter how discouraging or difficult—I feel better and more equipped to handle it after I exercise. By making my physical and mental well-being a priority, I keep myself in fighting shape—able to handle the pressures, demands, and commitments of a life of activism.

Daily exercise works for me, but it's important to find your own strategies to calm down, rest, and reenergize. Make them part of your everyday routine. Walks or runs in nature or around the neighborhood can clear your mind and balance out the stresses of the day. Meditating, journaling, or any kind of mindfulness activity—hiking, biking, yoga, or whatever works for you—can help you release tension and prevent burnout.

It's true that activism can sometimes feel like lonely work, with struggles few people understand. That's why it's also important to find others to talk to—family, friends, colleagues, or a professional therapist. It's never healthy to keep your emotions and anxieties to yourself. I check in frequently with a circle of people who know me really well—my wife, my sister, and a close friend I can call at any time of the day or night if I'm feeling worried or worn out. Professional therapists have also helped me manage the stress and anxiety I've felt when I've been under attack.

It's equally important to do things you enjoy that have nothing at all to do with your work as an activist. I like to change mental channels by reading a good book, being in nature, or watching a good movie or TV series. Hanging out with loved ones, having a good laugh, and spending time on hobbies and interests you enjoy are all ways to take your mind off daily pressures. It's easy to feel isolated or hyperfocused on our efforts to make change, but there's a whole world out there that has nothing to do with our work. It's important to be part of that and enjoy our lives as multidimensional human beings. Life is more than activism, and we have to remember that.

FOCUS ON CARE

Many activists began realizing the importance of self-care decades ago, in the 1960s and '70s. Rosa Parks, the civil rights activist who became famous in 1955 for refusing to sit at the back of a bus in Montgomery, Alabama, knew the importance of exercise for easing physical and mental stress. She grew up stretching and exercising with her mother, who was a teacher, and she later took up yoga so enthusiastically that she demonstrated poses at public events.[1]

In the 1970s, the Black Panther Party made self-care, preventive care, and access to medical treatment a priority in its outreach to the Black community. One of its leaders, Ericka Huggins, became a devotee of meditation and yoga while she was in prison for two years. "It saved me," she later recounted. "I thought I would spend the rest of my life incarcerated . . . I knew I had to make the best of it." Yoga and meditation, she said, "helped me in every nook and cranny of my life" and became a lifelong practice for her. "I meditate every day," she wrote.

> By sitting still in reflection, in prayer or in meditation, in small kindnesses, in feeding the hungry, in teaching a child, in facing the coinciding realities of all living beings—through spiritual practice—we open. When I recognize the love inside a human heart, even as the darkness struggles to gain power, I can breathe more easily, I have hope.[2]

Rest is also crucial to resilience and recovery from the pressures and anxieties of public advocacy. In the 1980s, Black activist and poet Audre Lord became a champion of self-care, which she saw as a political act. She reflected, "I am learning to balance stress with periods of rest and restoration. . . . I respect the time I spend each day treating my body, and I consider it part of my political work."[3]

More recently, poet, performance artist, and activist Tricia Hersey has promoted rest as a form of resistance and social justice, given the history of Black sleep deprivation and exhaustion since the era of slavery. In 2016, she founded the Nap Ministry, and she describes herself as the Nap Bishop.

"We have been taught to hustle, fake it till we make it, ignore our bodies' cues for rest," she explained in her book *Rest Is Resistance: A Manifesto*, "all because our systems have been created to ignore and push the laborers and the workers as hard as possible." But it's crucial, she added, to simply stop and feel.

> Can you remember a moment in your life when you have been told that the machine pace of your days is not normal? Sit with this for a moment. Breathe this in for a moment now. There has been no space for any of us to . . . hear the simple and bold proclamation, "You are doing too much. You can rest. You can just be." . . . Before experiencing this revelation, I believed that I had to figure out everything in my internal and external life that was causing me harm and correct it immediately with the information I had in front of me. Things were always urgent and rushed . . . I was never taught that I had a wealth of healing information and guidance waiting for me in a slowed-down state. . . . Urgency is a myth that preys upon your fears about the future.[4]

As these activists discovered, self-care builds resilience, strengthens body and soul, and makes it possible to overcome personal and political challenges, no matter how discouraging or daunting. It's essential to the success and sustainability of a life committed to social change.

UNPLUG AND UNWIND

Part of the challenge, these days, is staying calm and focused when you're bombarded by social media alerts, news, and notifications at every turn. It's too easy to get sucked into a habit of constant online connection, afraid that you'll miss something important or anxious for the validation of likes and shares. While it's helpful to check in and stay informed, it's just as crucial to check out and unplug on a regular basis to avoid feeling exhausted and triggered by too much incoming information, as well as online comments that might get negative or nasty.

As a well-known activist, I have been criticized a lot on social media, sometimes on an hourly basis. And some of those comments are viciously personal. It's easy to take these attacks personally and get outraged and demoralized by them. But I remind myself that those critics don't actually know me. They've never met me and have no clue what I'm about. So it's important to set boundaries. If online (or real-life) trolls come after you, tune them out, block them, and set social media limits and timeouts for yourself. Their attacks are not about you personally. You're an agent for a cause, and that can make you a target. Instead of dwelling on the negative comments, use social media conversations about the issues you care about to build a community of allies.

Better yet, step away from the clamor and clutter whenever you can. Unsubscribe from the deluge of ads and unwanted emails that clog your inbox. Unplug, shut down, and unwind on a regular basis to keep your emotional balance and your peace of mind.

Phones, especially, are such a focal part of our lives that it's easy to become addicted. That's why I make a point of keeping my phone out of the bedroom when I go to sleep. I don't want it buzzing or lighting up, so I purposely put it in another room. During the workday, I try to check it only once in a while, and I remind myself that I don't have to respond to texts and emails right away. As a religious Jew, I also literally unplug for twenty-five hours every week—from sunset on Friday until sunset on Saturday, during the Jewish Sabbath or Shabbat. That means no internet, no social media, no phone, and no screens, period. It's a terrific way to detox.

That's what filmmaker, artist, and author Tiffany Shlain discovered when she first tried it as an experiment with her family. I should note that she and her husband are both professionally immersed in technology all the time. Shlain is founder of the International Academy of Digital Arts and Sciences and cofounder of the Webby Awards, which honor excellence in digital media, and her husband, Ken Goldberg, is a robotics professor. But it all became too much. As Shlain explained in her book, *24/6: The Power of Unplugging One Day a Week*, "I was on screen 24/7. While I loved the power of having the world at my fingertips, I felt powerless against the allure of the device in my hand. Screens both consumed most of my time and made me lose track of it. . . . Most important, I felt like I wasn't paying enough attention to the people I loved who were right in front of me."

So she, Goldberg, and their two young daughters began a practice of shutting off all screens and unplugging for one full day each week. They were amazed at how reenergizing and refreshing it was. "Going screen-free . . . turns your life back *on*," she reflected. Once a week is ideal, she recommended, but even if you only do it every few weeks or months, it will enhance your life.[5]

GET OFF THE EMOTIONAL ROLLERCOASTER

Activism is a marathon, not a sprint. Social change, especially, can be a long, grueling process, and you may not see immediate results. Dealing with that can be tough, and there's a saying in activism: "If you're not overwhelmed, you're not paying attention." That often seems to be true. But if you regularly feel overwhelmed, you can become emotionally burned out, unable to continue the work needed to advance your cause. Given our society's focus on quick results, it's easy for activists to feel depressed, even hopeless, when they can't point to progress. But you have to pace yourself and keep your expectations realistic. Sometimes, the challenge is about changing cultural attitudes, and that can take years or even decades.[6]

I learned that when we founded a program called Transitions to Work that helps companies employ young adults with disabilities. It was an economic model designed to address the disproportionately high unemployment rate in a population that has untapped talent and boundless potential. Unfortunately, people with disabilities often face temporary placements, low wages, and limited work hours. Their high unemployment and underemployment rate is not merely a "disability issue" but a civil rights issue that impacts one of the largest minority groups in the country.

Transitions to Work has achieved a lot. Our twelve-week job training programs for young adults with disabilities produce job-ready, qualified candidates for appropriate positions. Our graduates earn jobs that provide good compensation and a sense of purpose. We engage employers as corporate partners, raise awareness about inclusive hiring, and provide ongoing employer and employee support. We have a placement rate of 70 percent, and job retention is very high.

Sounds like a success story, right? Unfortunately, the problem has been changing the mindset of employers. The business community continues to see the hiring of people with disabilities as charity. Of course, it's much more than that, with benefits for both employers and employees. Adults with disabilities can be fully qualified, committed candidates for appropriate employment opportunities. But changing hiring attitudes has been an uphill battle, and progress is difficult to measure. As with other cultural issues like tobacco use and marriage equality, it can take a long time to change social attitudes. But at some unpredictable point—after long-term, sustained effort—they can begin to shift.

For activists engaged in social change, it's important to know that you might not see results right away—or even, perhaps, in your own lifetime. But that doesn't make your efforts less meaningful and important. So pace yourself, keep your eyes on the goal, and don't give in to cynicism and self-doubt. Make sure you're rested and ready for the long haul.

COLLECTIVE CARE

It's also important to encourage a culture of care in your community. That's something that the Black Panthers emphasized. In early 1969, for example, the group started a free breakfast program for school-children in Oakland, California. The program was so successful that it was soon required in every Black Panther chapter across the country and fed more than twenty thousand schoolchildren a day.

The program was led by activist Ruth Beckford, who also used her training as a professional dancer to nurture and care for young girls in her community. As the founder and director of the U.S.'s first recreational dance program within Oakland's Parks and Recreation Department, Ruth provided free classes for students of all abilities, and she used those classes to mentor and build the confidence of girls. Her philosophy, she explained, was to "get them in through dance, but my whole goal was to make them be strong, free spirits. The girls got a lot of doses of self-empowerment training, self-esteem training. Out of the thousands of girls that I taught, I knew a few would be dancers, but they all had to become women. I wanted them all to be strong young ladies—and it worked."[7]

For Ruth Beckford, collective care was the core of her commitment to social change, and she literally changed lives. The philosophy of collective care is also important to building a team of activists who work well together over time. It can involve strategies like flexible and remote work, team gatherings and celebrations, and opportunities for support, fun, community, and education.[8]

Activist organizations are increasingly adopting and integrating this approach of caring for their people as the first step in caring for their cause. A few actually have "Happiness Engineers" on staff, whose job is to remind teammates to take care of their physical and emotional well-being. Other groups have taken a comprehensive approach to healthy activism. One of them, a nonprofit in Uganda called Raising Voices, is committed to personal reflection and support. Founded by Lori Michau and Dipak Naker in 1991 to prevent violence against women and children, Raising Voices embraces the idea that the social change they seek to inspire in others has to begin with themselves. The leaders of Raising Voices put it this way:

> The work we do in communities is intensely personal—we implore women and men, girls and boys to question the status quo; to reflect on their lives, on their relationships, and on their choices; and to envision a different way of being. This can't be achieved within communities if we don't first (and continually) undergo similar processes ourselves. Doing so requires an investment of time and resources at an organizational level as well as courage and vulnerability on a personal level. These efforts strengthen our work. We have learned that by exploring power

and justice in our own lives, we become more
attuned to the complexities of injustice, more skilled
in helping others through processes, and more committed to seeing change.[9]

In short, they strive to support each other first as they work to
achieve progress in the wider community. To explore the importance of support, Raising Voices surveyed more than 260 activists
who work on the issue of violence against women, to see how
they were doing and understand their hopes, struggles, and concerns. They learned that many activists felt inspired, hopeful, and
engaged, while others felt tired, worried, and discouraged about
the work and their own well-being. Burnout was a major concern,
as was the lack of self-care and time for recharge and recovery.
Many stressed the importance of kindness and compassion to one-
self and one's colleagues, and of nurturing one another's mental,
physical, and emotional health.

Raising Voices has made a point of prioritizing self- and collective care so that their activists have the physical and emotional
stamina and resilience to do their work. It's about modeling, they
say, a balance of "head and heart, skills and spirit—knowing that
such a balance will bring our practice to new levels." In the end, they
add, "the work is only as good as the people leading the effort."[10]

Bottom line, if you don't take care of yourself, you will limit
your ability to help others. Activism is tough work, and to do it
sustainably and well, you have to stay in strong physical, mental,
and emotional shape. Taking care of your own well-being is not

at all a self-centered distraction. Instead, it's a requirement of success. So find your own strategies for keeping your mind and body healthy, rested, and resilient. Turn off your phone, step away from screens, and unplug as often as you can. Limit your exposure to toxic people—online and in real life. Pace yourself. Don't give in to cynicism and self-doubt. And take care of your community and team. By finding ways to relax and recharge, keeping your expectations realistic, and finding a community for support, you can keep moving the ball forward, day by day.

CHAPTER 8

KNOW YOUR NO

"The art of leadership is saying no, not saying yes.
It is very easy to say yes."

—TONY BLAIR, former prime minister
of the United Kingdom

Sometimes, the healthiest decision you can make is to press pause and take a time-out. If the stress and conflict of activism overwhelms your personal sense of balance and starts undermining your physical and mental health, it's time to say no for a while and take a break. Burnout, anxiety, and exhaustion can erode your energy, enthusiasm, effectiveness, and judgment—qualities that are essential for activists. So before you hit the wall, it's best to walk away, rest up, and focus on your mental and physical health so you can come back recharged.

A key step is setting boundaries. No activist has to do everything. Perhaps you feel most comfortable and competent working as an organizer or researcher behind the scenes. Or maybe you thrive when you're out front, speaking to the public and the press, and dislike the details of planning a campaign or event. You do not have to do it all. Focus on the work you're best at and find most rewarding and say no to the rest. Others on your team with a complementary set of skills can fill in.

One of the best examples of saying no and stepping back was when gymnast Simone Biles, a four-time Olympic gold medalist, dropped out of the 2020 Tokyo Olympics early because the stress of competition was threatening her mental and physical sense of balance. At twenty-four, Biles was an extraordinary athlete who hadn't lost a single competition in the all-around category since she was sixteen. She was expected to win at least three more gold medals in Tokyo. But suddenly, while performing a vault during an Olympic event, she couldn't gauge where her body was in space or where the ground was. Biles was experiencing the "twisties," a confounding sense of physical disorientation gymnasts can feel when they're under stress. Biles realized that her mind and her body were not in sync, and that she was at risk of injuring herself badly.

So she decided to say no to further competitions and dropped out. "'Simone,'" she told herself, "'it's okay. It's not the end of the world . . . If you walk away from this and you still are walking, that's a win in your book.'" It was, she later judged, "probably the most courageous I've ever been." For the first time in her life, she said, she had to prioritize her own welfare. "That's why we have teammates," she added, "because if somebody's feeling down, you have to step up. And they did just that."

Saying no, for Biles, was unquestionably the right decision. After putting her physical and mental health first for two years, she returned to competition at the top of her game. She went on to win her eighth straight all-around title in the national championships, four gold medals in the world championships, and a lifetime total of thirty-seven medals—more than any gymnast in history. By saying no, she stood up as an activist for mental health and led by example.[1]

SAY NO TO PEOPLE YOU DON'T TRUST

As Biles knows, teamwork is essential to success—in athletics as well as activism. That's why building alliances is so important. But here's a rule I always follow: don't work with any people or organizations you don't trust. Your priorities won't be aligned, or they may try to take advantage of your hard work, contacts, and ideas for their own agenda. If you get the wrong feeling from somebody, even if they're working on the same issue, say no and walk away.

I've learned that lesson from experience. Years ago, when we first started our campaign for greater inclusion and representation of disability in TV and movies, we decided to host a conference on the issue at the Four Seasons Hotel in Beverly Hills. It would be the first large-scale event on disabilities and entertainment, and many show runners, actors, producers, and other important industry people were going to attend. We were putting in a ton of work and getting a lot of media attention. But just days before the conference, the leader of an allied group asked us to postpone it so it wouldn't compete with an event on inclusion that *Variety*, the influential industry magazine, was planning to host—because apparently, the *Variety* event had decided at the last minute to include the issue of disability and entertainment. I concluded that this bizarre request, which was made via a mass email, was this untrustworthy ally's way of trying to bully me. As you can imagine, I said no to postponing our conference. And by the way, we later hosted a very successful event in partnership with *Variety* that focused on disability inclusion and representation.[2]

The point is, you should pick your partners carefully. Good alliances are built on mutual support and trust. If someone is not offering that, walk away. And say no to anyone who wants to use you for their own purposes. That's why I decline a lot of honors and awards. I know that many of the groups who want to present them to me are mainly hoping to gain my support and partnership. They are hoping that I will introduce them to people and help them raise money for their own issues, which may not match up with mine. So bottom line, even if your goals seem similar, be cautious about aligning yourself too closely with potential allies. Build a big tent, but don't bring people into it whom you don't trust. Know their agenda and make sure you're comfortable with it. No matter how highly recommended they are by other people, and no matter how helpful you think they might be to your goals as an activist—be careful. If something about their judgment or behavior seems off, listen to your gut.

KNOW YOUR VALUES

Like anyone, I also periodically engage in battles with myself about the nature and necessity of compromise. On the one hand, compromise can build relationships. On the other hand, it can shrink your goals, dwindle your dreams, undermine your values, and effectively sell your soul to the very system you're fighting.

Sometimes you have to say no and take a stand. I know I personally have the ability to walk away from any situation that imperils my values. For example, I've chosen a different path from many of my fellow foundation heads. Most philanthropists confine their efforts to choosing nonprofit organizations they deem worthy of support and writing checks to help them. Obviously, that work is beneficial, but its transactional nature has never satisfied me. In my opinion, our broken world demands putting in your own work and putting yourself on the line to take a stand. Donors are important to funding causes, but activism is about more than money. And I dislike the perceived necessity in many nonprofit organizations of pleasing donors first. Ego and elitism also lie at the root of many troubled relationships in philanthropies, nonprofits, and elsewhere. They can sometimes supersede the organizations' values and agendas and devalue those who do the essential work on which their constituents rely.

You can see it in some organizations' elitist pecking order—their assumption that a board member does X, a staffer does Y, and so on, in a descending "order of importance" that I find intolerable. It reminds me of an interaction I once had with a billionaire philanthropist. "If I were willing to live lower on the food chain," he told me, "I'd become a teacher." Talk about elitist. In fact, I once resigned from a seat on the board of an organization because of its elitist culture and behavior. Afterward, Shira asked me, "Why are you always walking away?" The answer is, it keeps me honest.

I've often thought about the principled stand that legendary heavyweight boxing champion Muhammad Ali took when he refused to be drafted into the U.S. military during the Vietnam War. Ali believed the war was immoral, so he stood his ground and took the consequences. Ali was stripped of his heavyweight titles, and in June 1967, he was sentenced to five years in federal prison. But he didn't relent, and his harsh punishment helped energize the antiwar movement. According to the late activist and Georgia state senator Julian Bond, Ali's stand "reverberated through the whole society . . . It was on everyone's lips. People who had never thought about the war before began to think it through because of Ali. The ripples were enormous"—on a global level, igniting pro-Ali protests around the world. Ali's conviction was finally overturned by the U.S. Supreme Court in 1971, but the boxer never regretted his decision.[3]

"Some people thought I was a hero," he said. "Some people said that what I did was wrong. But everything I did was according to my conscience."[4] As the Black civil rights activist, poet, and philosopher Audre Lord once forcefully declared, "I have come to believe over and over again that what is most important to me must be spoken, made verbal and shared, even at the risk of having it bruised or misunderstood."[5]

At some point, as individuals and activists, most of us have to face a decision regarding a system or relationship that threatens to either compromise our principles or weaken our cause. I realized that if

I wanted to continue to push for my cause, it would require me to come out as a critic or take a stand that would piss people off. I had to get comfortable with being unpopular—and I've discovered I'm rather good at it. Relationships matter. But the unpopularity I'm willing to embrace as an advocate for those causes—my ability to say no to what I consider to be toxic compromise—has proven to be an effective dimension of my activist practice. As the late English author and minimum-wage advocate Alfred George Gardiner observed, one person with conviction can "overwhelm a hundred who have only opinions." That person won't necessarily be popular at parties or have the most followers on social media. But they will have the potential to change minds and help create a new world.

SAY NO TO MISSION CREEP

As I've discussed, the most effective way for activists to define the scope of their issue is to go narrow and deep. In our case, we've been very focused on the issue of disability inclusion. We've also shifted into the related issue of mental health. Both are issues that keep people from participating fully in life and society. We strategically adapted our mission to include mental health because of its enormous impact and the chronic lack of resources available to address it.

But strategic adaptation is very different from "mission creep"— the unplanned expansion of a mission beyond its original scope. Mission creep is a big problem for many activists who start advocating for one issue, then get pulled into others without much reflection or consideration. Now, I'm not talking about giving time or making a small donation when a friend asks you to contribute to a cause or charity that is not your focus. Those small acts of generosity honor your friendship and help you nurture your own community. But it's important not to overcommit to causes that are not your own. They will only sap your energy and resources and dilute your impact.

If you're an environmental activist, for example, it might also be tempting to take public stands on reproductive health, gun control, or other causes. I know that many activists will disagree with me on this, but here's my strong advice: don't do it. If you put your name to all these other causes, you will end up driving away some who support your core environmental mission, you will overstretch your human and financial resources, and you will erode your brand—with very little to show for it. So say no to those who want to enlist you in causes that have little to do with your core mission, and be very strategic about issues that you do take on.

You can care about other issues. You can give money or time to them, but don't mix them in with your activism. This is about elevating your cause. It's okay to have other interests, but in order to not dilute your power and the brand you are creating, you'll want to avoid mission creep.

WHEN TO KNOW YOUR NO

It can be hard to resist the pressure to say yes—to tasks you feel expected to do, to potential allies and partners who seem enthusiastic about your cause, to compromise for the sake of benefits, or to issues that are popular but unrelated to your core mission. But do practice saying no. In many cases, for an activist, it's the best response.

How do you know when no is the right answer? Here are six signs that should raise red flags and make you step on the brakes:

1. **You feel burned out, anxious, and exhausted.** You have pushed yourself beyond your physical and mental limit. It's time to stop, step away, and tend to your health before you damage yourself.

2. **You don't feel comfortable with a potential ally.** Listen to your gut. If there's anything that seems untrustworthy about that individual or organization, walk away.

3. **A partner is not treating you as an equal.** That's a sign that your relationship is transactional and imbalanced. You are not being supported—you are being used. Say no.

4. **The chemistry of your relationship no longer feels positive, even though you've tried to work on it.** The partnership has probably run its course. It is time to move on.

5. **You are asked to compromise your values.** Always say no to anything that goes against your core values. If you can't stand up for your own beliefs and convictions, how can you fight effectively for your cause?

6. **You are asked to speak out about unrelated causes.** Don't do it. You may personally feel strongly about a lot of issues, but keep your public activism focused on your core mission. Otherwise, you'll diminish the impact of your work and support for the issue that you care most about.

Know the power of no. It's one of the secrets of successful advocacy.

CHAPTER 9

TAKE THE WIN . . . THEN KEEP FIGHTING

"Get up, stand up: don't give up the fight!"
—BOB MARLEY, Jamaican singer

Activism isn't something we should endure. Instead, it's something to celebrate, repeatedly, for big accomplishments as well as minor gains. I frequently remind my team that our work is about doing good, but it's also about bringing joy into our lives. I think that's something we tend to overlook. The challenges we face are tough, and we often get caught up in the painful conditions and inequities we're trying to address. But by celebrating success, no matter how small—and doing it collectively, with those you work with—you can keep your spirits and motivation high and keep striving together for the next win.

Truthfully, I get my greatest joy from the relationships I form through activism. For me, it's wonderful to have success, but it's even better to meet the people who help me get there. I'm actually often surprised when we have a win. For example, when Major League Baseball changed the name of its "Disabled List" to the "Injured List," I was amazed, especially at how quickly it happened. That was because people in the MLB—especially the late Billy Bean, its Senior Vice President of Diversity, Equity, and Inclusion—clearly understood the need for change. Bean and others didn't resist it, and they made it happen. When ViacomCBS, NBCUniversal, Paramount, and Sony Pictures Entertainment each issued announcements committing to disability inclusion, I was also overjoyed. Those changes also happened because people inside the studios understood and supported the changes we asked for.

Successes like these are reminders that there are good people in the world, and that is also something to celebrate. We do it publicly, through the Morton E. Ruderman Award in Inclusion and the Ruderman Seal of Approval for Authentic Representation. But however you do it—by popping a bottle of champagne, ordering a pizza for your team, or high-fiving and dancing around your desks—successes, and the joys of effective and persistent effort, are something to share.

AMPLIFYING VOICES OF POSITIVE CHANGE

For a young Israeli-Palestinian named Nuseir Yassin, joy actually *is* activism. In 2016, after graduating from Harvard and working

for a time at Venmo, Yassin began traveling the globe and pro-
ducing a one-minute video a day for a thousand days. That's an
astounding one thousand videos focused on the good around
the world, from African villages to the skyscrapers of Singapore.
Yassin was determined to travel widely, to meet real people in
their home environments, and to share the stories of those who
are striving to make the world better. He uploaded these sixty-
second videos to his *Nas Daily* page on Facebook, where they've
been seen by millions.

For Yassin, it was about more than video-making. He was committed to being a force for good—bringing people together, focusing
on positivity, and sharing stories of people, companies, and organizations that are doing their part to make life better. His quest, he
explained, was a reaction to his own experience growing up as a
Palestinian in Israel.

> I wanted *Nas Daily* to be the opposite of what I saw
> growing up—wars between Israel and Hezbollah
> and Israel and Hamas. I saw people labeling them-
> selves—"I'm Jewish," "I'm Muslim," "I'm Black,"
> "I'm White," "I'm Bedouin," "I'm a farmer." I saw
> a lot of casting, I saw a lot of turmoil, and I saw a
> lot of negativity in the news every single day. And
> if something bad happens in the world, there are
> at least ten thousand organizations that are ready
> to talk about it and make it a bigger deal. They're
> ready to publicize it in the news and the media. But
> there is no one who is ready to tell you what's going

well in the world—what is happening that's inspiring, that is positive.

That's what I wanted *Nas Daily* to be. It's almost the antidote to what exists today. It's not just kumbaya positivity—"let's all be friends, this is great." It's more about amplifying actionable, real, positive impact that is happening now—stories that smart people and kids who are ten years old can enjoy watching.

And they are watching. After Yassin uploaded his first thousand daily videos, his page had four billion views and thirteen million followers. *Nas Daily* was a global phenomenon.

Since then, Yassin has created a training program for video creators called Nas Academy. He wants to teach what he has learned along the way and help give aspiring creators a much-needed boost. His hope is to inspire youth and encourage them to make their own positive changes in the world. His mission, he said, "is to leave a net positive mark, no matter how small or big." And he loves to share and celebrate his success.

"I figured out how to make a video," he said, and "I'm going to tell the world about it. My belief is that the more you share about your success, the more success you will create in the world. I think it becomes a moral imperative, a moral responsibility, to share how you did it, because we want more *Nas Dailies* in the world, not less. The world does not need one *Nas Daily*," he explained. "It needs a hundred."[1]

WIN OR LOSE, KEEP FIGHTING

Successes are wonderful, but they can feel all too rare. As an activist, you will win some battles, and you will lose others. But don't get discouraged, and don't give up. Remember—persistence and perseverance are essential because change rarely happens overnight. And, unfortunately, wins can sometimes turn into losses.

One painful example is the right to choose. The overturning of *Roe v. Wade* in 2022 shattered nearly fifty years of legal precedent and withdrew a fundamental right from American citizens, one they had enjoyed since 1973. Americans won the right to reproductive freedom that year, after decades of abortions being criminally banned in a majority of states. The Supreme Court's shocking 2022 decision in *Dobbs v. Jackson Women's Health Organization* revoked that cherished legal freedom to decide when and if to become a parent, as well as access to appropriate health care for many women whose lives and well-being are put at risk by pregnancy.[2]

The Supreme Court issued its devastating decision, but the fight for reproductive rights is not over by any means. Activists are more committed than ever to fight on: telling stories that humanize the abortion issue, helping women navigate the increasingly perilous landscape of their rights and health, working to keep pharmaceutical abortions legal and widely available, and helping women travel to safe-harbor states to obtain abortions. Crucial battles have moved to courtrooms, state legislatures, and ballot boxes across the country, as other activists work to boost voter engagement and turnout in support of referenda and candidates that will preserve the right to choose and push for federal laws to guarantee that right across the nation.[3]

Sometimes you fail, sometimes you go backward, and progress can feel next to impossible, but don't stop fighting for the issues and values you believe in. Climate activists, too, can feel overwhelmed by the size and stakes of the challenges they face trying to curb or arrest global warming. According to a recent survey, more than half of all young people in countries around the world feel anxious, sad, angry, and powerless about the prospects of climate change, while older people worry about its effects on their children and grand-children's futures. But despite the immensity of the challenge, many have become climate activists—doing whatever they can, in private or collective ways, to make a difference. Even when you can only see incremental progress and your goal seems almost impossibly hard to achieve, don't stop working and fighting for solutions.[4]

The fact is, progress rarely happens in a straight line. It zigzags. In my own experience, despite years of successful activism in dis-ability inclusion and representation, movies are still coming out that feature disabled characters portrayed by actors who do not have disabilities. It is frustrating and at times infuriating. For example, when *Wonka* came out with Hugh Grant inauthentically playing a little person, I cringed.[5] But since films are cast and made years before we see them, progress will always appear gradual. But there's no reason to be discouraged or inhibited by setbacks. You have to keep at it, trying new strategies and tactics. In my case, these days, that means praising the industry when they do get it right instead of publicly criticizing studios for every stumble.

YOU ARE RUNNING A LONG RACE

Of course, it takes a lot of internal fortitude to keep working for the greater good when the odds seem against you. People have different strengths and skill sets, so activism isn't the right path for everyone. Some people, though, seem born to keep fighting on the front lines.

Take Amariyanna "Mari" Copeny of Flint, Michigan, for example. In 2015, when she was just seven years old, Copeny was named "Little Miss Flint" because of her proposal to build ties between children and local police officers. The next year, when she was eight, she turned her attention to a very serious crisis facing both children and adults in her community. In April 2014, in an effort to save money, Michigan officials changed Flint's source of drinking water from Lake Huron and the Detroit River to the Flint River. But they didn't properly treat the water, which contained harmful levels of bacteria and corroded Flint's aging water pipes, which leached lead into the city's water supply.[6]

The drinking water, Copeny said, "smelled funny, and it was brown. It wasn't something you'd want to drink." It also caused reported health problems, including hair loss and skin reactions. Copeny and her family could only take showers for two minutes before the water started to irritate their skin, causing rashes. Although they tried to limit their exposure, Copeny still has scars on her arms from the Flint water. Lead exposure is also a grave concern. A hundred thousand Flint residents, including eight thousand children, have been exposed to high lead levels, which can lead to long-term developmental and health problems. And bacteria in the Flint River water caused an outbreak of

Legionnaires' disease, a severe form of pneumonia, that led to the death of twelve people.[7]

When the water quality deteriorated, eight-year-old Copeny wanted to do something, anything, to help. According to her mother, LuLu Brezzell, "When we started hearing about the crisis, she felt like she wanted to speak up. So she started dragging us out to go to all of these meetings, rallies, and protests." Copeny and her mother even planned to travel to Washington, DC, to watch the congressional testimony of Michigan's governor, Rick Snyder. Before they left, Copeny decided to write a letter to President Obama asking if she could possibly meet with him while she was in the capital:[8]

> Mr. President,
>
> Hello my name is Mari Copeny and I'm 8 years old, I live in Flint, Michigan, and I'm more commonly known around town as "Little Miss Flint." I am one of the children that is effected by this water, and I've been doing my best to march in protest and to speak out for all the kids that live here in Flint. This Thursday I will be riding a bus to Washington, D.C. to watch the congressional hearings of our Governor Rick Snyder. I know this is probably an odd request but I would love for a chance to meet you or your wife. My mom said chances are you will be too busy with more important things, but there is a lot of people coming on these buses and even just a meeting from you or your wife would really

lift people's spirits. Thank you for all that [you] do for our country. I look forward to being able to come to Washington and to be able to see Gov. Snyder in person and to be able to be in the city where you live.

Thank You
Mari Copeny

President Obama wrote back that "letters from kids like you are what make me so optimistic about the future." And although he said that he couldn't meet her in Washington, he planned to travel to Flint and meet with her there. He did so the next month. He even mentioned Mari Copeny in a speech he gave in Flint, while she stood right behind him on stage.

Obama authorized the Federal Emergency Management Agency (FEMA) to provide water, water filters, water filter cartridges, water test kits, and other important items to supplement the state and local response to Flint's water crisis and directed the Environmental Protection Agency (EPA) and Centers for Disease Control (CDC) to investigate. And his response to young Copeny's request was beyond anything she could have imagined. "I didn't expect anything when I sent the letter," she recalled. "I didn't even think he would write back. I thought I was being pranked when I heard he wanted to meet me. But it was the greatest, awesomest, most epic experience of my life."[9]

Since then, there has been a major effort to replace the lead service lines in Flint, Michigan, with $400 million in state and federal funding dedicated to the project. But many residents—who had been advised to use only bottled water for years—are still staying away from tap water.

"Lead levels have reached 'safe' levels," Copeny explained, "but at least at my house we are having huge issues with the extra chemicals they are treating the water with." Although her family has a filter for the shower, the water, after a couple of minutes, "still burns our eyes, the water still gives us rashes that look like chemical burns, and we still can't take baths. We are still using bottled water for everything we consume. It is scary," she added, "because I don't know what is going to happen to me or the other kids from Flint. I am just trying to stay alive."[10]

And she is still working to help. She and the Michigan-based education nonprofit Pack Your Back have provided more than 700,000 water bottles to families in the community. And Copeny is using her activism to help local kids in other ways.

"When people think of Flint," she noted, "they sometimes only remember the water crisis and not that there are kids here that need some extra love and attention. Everything I do is to help out, lift, and inspire Flint kids to know they are better than the water crisis; that they are loved, remembered, and real-life superheroes."

So Copeny does everything in her own power to make a difference. Her efforts include a "Dear Flint Kids" letter-writing campaign that she started to bring letters of encouragement from around the world to Flint children. In 2017, she raised $18,000 and partnered with a nonprofit to throw a Christmas party for five hundred kids and give out thousands of toys. She arranged free screenings of *Black Panther* and had more than a thousand copies of Madeleine L'Engle's *A Wrinkle in Time* donated so that kids, she explained, "can read the book and enjoy the magic that comes with reading." Copeny also supported a local anti-bullying non-profit, made Easter baskets for kids in need, and started a "Don't Forget Flint" shirt campaign to help fund many of her small projects.[11] Partnering with Pack Your Back, she also raised funds to fill fifteen thousand backpacks with everything that local students need for school, including pens, pencils, markers, crayons, highlighters, books, and notebooks.

By the time Copeny was sixteen, she had addressed audiences in front of the White House and at the United Nations. She was also named the youngest Youth Ambassador for the Women's March, as well as Youth Ambassador for the Climate March and Equality for Her. But Mari Copeny is still a kid—a cheerleader and artist who loves comic books, superhero movies, Pokémon, and American Girl Dolls. "I love to draw," she added. "I love to read. I love to eat. I love spending time with my friends. I love tap dance just as much as I love cheer. I love video games. I love all kinds of music."

And she is likely an activist for life. Copeny recalls, "My mom told me going in that a lot of times my words would not be heard, and I would have to work twenty times harder than most adults because I am a kid, and adults just don't take kids seriously." But, Copeny stressed, "I think it is important for youth to be engaged, especially now, with politicians messing with our futures and our lives before we are even old enough to vote. It is good to know that one simple march or protest won't create instant change; it's more of a kickoff to a longer race to get the change we want to see. It may seem hard and feel like you're being ignored but know that the more you speak up and use your voice, people will start to listen."[12]

STAY THE COURSE

Mari Copeny's activism didn't solve the Flint water crisis, but it helped to bring attention to the problem. Your activism may not achieve your goals; success might not even come in your lifetime. But your efforts can still move the ball, and that's the important thing.

Celebrate the wins—don't take them for granted. But know that there will always be ups and downs and change often takes time. In my own life, I remember when smoking was considered cool. It took decades of activism, on many fronts, before there was a sea change in social mores and smoking became frowned upon. Legislation, of course, was part of that, but the real fight was for people's hearts and minds. It often takes a while for people to get it, but they do.

That's where you can make a difference, daily, as an activist. Keep speaking up about the issues that are important to you. Don't be afraid to tell people what you believe. Do what you can to make positive change, in a way that's right for you, and don't give up when you lose a round.

Take a breath, take a beat, then get back in the ring. The only time you truly lose is when you give up.

CHAPTER 10

STAY FLEXIBLE

"The sign of intelligence is the ability to change."
—ALBERT EINSTEIN, theoretical physicist

T ime passes and things change. You have to accept that change is a constant. Society, demographics, technology, and the world never stand still, and as an activist, you have to keep up. Don't get stuck in your ways.

So follow the news, follow your issue, and keep up with what's going on. Adapt your message and how to get it out to stay effective. If your message and methods don't evolve, they will become dated.

Over the years, I've changed how I've gotten my message out many times. When I started in political campaigns, I was printing flyers and going door to door. Then I started blogging every week as a way to keep people informed. When blogging became less relevant, I started podcasting as a way to reach more people. Maybe

Instagram, Facebook, or X (formerly known as Twitter) work best for you. Do whatever feels right and suits your skill set. But the important thing is to keep experimenting with and adopting new tools as the world changes. Don't let your activism get stale.

SAME ISSUES, DIFFERENT CHALLENGES

The focus of activism also changes with different times and generations. In the 1960s, activists succeeded in moving the ball forward in civil rights, and the 1970s saw gains for feminists, reproductive rights, gay rights, the environment—but those struggles are not over by any measure. Young people and activists today are still facing those same issues and, in some cases, progress has been reversed. The fight continues, but the tools and the focus have changed.[1]

The 2020 murder of George Floyd by a white police officer in Minneapolis—witnessed by millions on TV and social media—motivated a whole new generation of activists to battle against structural racism. In the 2017 national Women's March, some five million people took to the streets to protest misogyny and threats to women's rights, and the 2022 overturning of *Roe v. Wade* only increased those stakes. Young activists today are on the front lines of the fight for gender equality and LGBTQ+ rights, and the disability rights movement has emerged as a growing civil rights issue. Climate change has also inspired a new wave of activists, with extreme weather becoming more urgent and dangerous than ever.

Today's young activists see these issues through their own lens, with a heightened awareness of crisis. Especially in the wake of the COVID-19 pandemic, young people have a sense of global instability, with impacts that directly affect their lives. In the past, environmental issues appeared abstract, but now it's personal. We know that if we don't start changing our behavior, our future and our kids' futures will be compromised. With rising sea levels and global temperatures, for example, parts of our world may well become uninhabitable if we don't change.[2]

Before 2022, it was also easy for young women to assume that their rights to reproductive freedom were a given. But the Supreme Court's decision in *Dobbs* eliminated those rights for more than twenty million Americans. Suddenly, that issue has become front and center for a new generation of activists, because it affects their lives. And when people think an issue has an impact on them, they care, and they speak out. According to one recent survey, as many as 70 percent of Gen Zers have become involved in social or political causes, and young people are entering activism at an earlier age.[3]

In India, for example, a young girl named Licypriya Kangujam became an activist at the age of seven. She stood outside the Indian parliament for a week, holding a sign that read, "Dear Mr. Modi and MPS, pass the climate change law and save our future." Because sea levels are rising and the Earth is becoming hotter, she demanded, "they should act now." The next year, at the age of eight, she launched the "Great October March 2019," inspiring thousands throughout India to march during one autumn week to demand immediate action on climate change and passage of the proposed climate law.[4] At ten, Kangujam started a cleanup campaign after she tweeted a photograph of mounds of plastic trash behind the Taj Mahal. In the photo, she held a sign that read, "Behind the beauty of the Taj Mahal is plastic pollution." Alongside this image, she tweeted, "Thanks humans . . . your [single-use] . . . polythene bag, one simple plastic water bottle led [to] this situation when millions of people visit every year."

As Kangujam explained to the press, "I found plastic waste including food wrappers and bottles inside the fountain and gardens of Taj Mahal. The area around the monument was littered with single-use plastics. This is really very bad. Such a dark side of the iconic landmark tarnishes the image of the country. Authorities must take strict cognizance of the matter." By sharing the picture, she said, she wanted "to send a strong, poignant message about environmental degradation and resilience to the whole world." And it worked. Authorities took action after she tweeted, and when Kangujam visited the site again, she reported, "it was almost entirely clean." Other young activists, like Mari Copeny, have stepped up as leaders for positive change, because they see their own lives and futures in the balance.[5]

Many ongoing battles are now being led by this new generation, bringing different skills, experiences, and perspectives to the fight. Older activists would be wise to ally themselves with younger advocates and adapt their causes and approaches to new times and tools. That's one of the reasons I started LINK20, a global social movement led by a network of young and tenacious activists, with and without disabilities, whose focus is social justice and inclusion. Their involvement and activism will carry our work forward.

SOCIAL MEDIA HAS EMPOWERED THE INDIVIDUAL

So much of this new surge of activism is enabled by social media. Digital technology instantly alerts us to news and social and political issues, giving them an immediacy they often lacked in the earlier era of newspapers and nightly news. With constant, 24/7 access to information and communication, young activists are motivated to act and can do so instantaneously, in direct and creative ways—sharing news, building and mobilizing their communities. You no longer need an army of leafletters, canvassers, and phone bankers to organize and elevate an issue. Individuals can do it easily themselves, and they have the real power to make change.

In 2023, for example, when a devastating red tide, caused by an algae bloom, struck the coast of Florida and killed millions of fish, a vlogger named Paul Cuffaro highlighted the disaster in a TikTok video that nearly six million people watched. News outlets then began reporting on the story, and millions more have been made aware of the problem, which was linked to human pollution.[6]

Social media has democratized and accelerated activism, putting the ability to have impact in the hands of any advocate, of any age. According to a 2020 survey, more than a third of eight-to-seventeen-year-olds said that online information motivated them to act on an issue, and nearly half believed that their voices made a difference. From #BlackLivesMatter and #MeToo to global movements for social justice, digital tools have made it easier than ever to take direct action and have an impact on the issues you care about—without the need for financial backing, resources, or connections.[7]

I don't think it's an overstatement to say that digital media has revolutionized and reanimated activism. It's a tool that has empowered people around the world, and it will continue to evolve. With looming advances in AI and technologies that we can't yet imagine, the power and shape of activism is sure to change.

And while many movements originated at the grassroots, they've gained potency as more advocates win access to political power. The "outsider" activism I've practiced has been fortified and amplified on the inside—by feminists, environmentalists, LGBTQ+ advocates, and others who have been voted into elective office or stepped into other positions of influence and authority in media, academia, and law. Morover, the battle today is often at the ballot box. There may be no clearer example of voter activism than in the wake of the *Dobbs* decision, with the success of pro-choice referenda in Ohio, Virginia, and Kentucky. With their reproductive rights and health at stake, individuals in all these states acted on the issue and cast their ballots to bring decisive wins in elections and public policy.[8]

MY ACTIVIST JOURNEY

I wasn't alive yet in 1961 when President John F. Kennedy famously said in his inaugural address, "Ask not what your country can do for you; ask what you can do for your country,"[9] but I took those words and the ideals they embodied to heart. The results of that commitment have filled these pages.

My family now lives in the Boston area, the birthplace of President Kennedy. Such is the circle of life, I guess, that after reading endlessly about the Kennedys as a boy, now as a middle-aged man I can take my dog for a walk and shortly arrive at the Beals Street National Historic Site, where John F. Kennedy was born. The values that motivated me to become an activist in college, inspired by Kennedy's call to service, still infuse my work for justice on a daily basis. While many aspects of activism have changed since those early days, others have not. My tactics, tools, and strategies have shifted, but my values and commitment haven't. They are my North Star.

Although you always have to grow, adapt, and learn in order to remain relevant, there are also fundamentals about activism that don't change. In this book I've illuminated those constants. The lessons I've discussed are ones that every activist should learn. They will help you be as effective as possible, and they're accessible to and achievable by every advocate. Let's go over them once more.

First, you need to find your fight. What is it that fuels your own passion for change? What's the issue that you care most about—the one that moves you in your heart and mind? That's the issue worth fighting for—because when you're acting from the heart, you have the power to move other people's hearts and minds and inspire them to join you in making change. Focus on the issue that you feel most deeply about and let that caring and commitment drive your activism. Authentic, heartfelt advocacy makes a powerful difference.

Start with persistence. Activism isn't easy. You may lose more often than you win, and progress can be incremental. That's why persistence is one of the most important qualities to bring to the fight. It's a long road, but if you keep moving forward step by step—even if you occasionally take a few steps backward—you'll likely succeed on a meaningful level. Just keep at it. Don't let yourself get discouraged. Keep your eye on the prize and keep fighting for progress, one step at a time.

Know your facts. You have to know what you're talking about if you want other people to listen to what you have to say. In fact, the more you know about your issue, the more persuasive you'll be. So spend the time to learn everything you can about your cause—its history and social, cultural, economic, and political impacts. Make a point of finding out who else is also working on your issue and consider whether you should become allies. Knowledge is unquestionably power when it comes to activism.

Foster your community. Making change is not a solo activity. One voice can call attention to a problem, but it takes many voices speaking together and calling for change to fix it. You need to work with others who can complement your skills and interests, and you need allies who bring their own platforms and supporters to the cause. By building a community of people who care about the same issues, you'll amplify and strengthen all your efforts to make positive change.

Court controversy. Make "good trouble," as the late Congressman John Lewis put it. Don't be afraid to criticize or confront power. Both are great ways to bring attention to your issue. When you create conflict in a public forum, you have an exceptional chance to capture people's interest and even change minds. And when you spark controversy with a media celebrity, you can bring your message to an audience of millions.

Leverage power. Criticism and controversy are effective, but after you've gotten people's attention, it's smart to leverage that notoriety to win allies on the inside—in government, organizations, and companies—who can help you achieve wins. As your partners in change, they can increase social pressure and wield their power on the inside to advance your issue.

Take care of yourself. All of this takes a lot of hard work and energy, and it can take a toll. But don't let activism exhaust you and burn you out. Make sure you pay attention to your well-being. Take breaks, switch gears, and find people you can talk to about any problems and struggles you're having. Taking care of yourself isn't a selfish distraction from activism. It's necessary if you're in it for the long haul and committed to keep fighting for the causes you believe in.

Know your no. If you do get burned out, you may have to step away from your activism for a while. Saying no can be a healthy, even necessary choice when it comes to preserving your mental and physical health. You should also say no to partnering with people you don't fully trust. Always listen to your gut and walk away from anything that threatens your health, your credibility, or your cause.

Take the win . . . then keep fighting. All your successes, both big and small, are worth celebrating. So be sure to take the time to mark those winning moments with your team. Since the work life of an activist is up and down, it's important to celebrate the ups. It fortifies your confidence and spirit. For sure, there will be down times, but that's okay. Just try to move the ball forward a little every day, and soon enough, there will be more successes to celebrate.

I've chosen activism as my vocation, and it's given me a great sense of satisfaction—humility, too. I'm both gratified and humbled by what my team has been able to accomplish in our fight for authentic representation. Our work is far from done, but we've had an impact.

One of the wonderful things I've learned about activism is that you eventually learn what works. And at this point in my career, I know an opportunity when I see it. I have a feel for when the media will pick something up, really seize on a story and circulate it, and create a public appetite for change.

Don't get me wrong—I still make mistakes. But the gains are potentially too great to be discouraged or inhibited by failure. Besides, when you choose your allies well, as I recommend you do, they will help you through your challenges, hold you to your goals, and keep the faith.

The future of activism is still being written. But I know that mastery and impact are about staying on the path and adapting your methods and messages to new times and tools. As an activist, I'm always evolving and exploring new issues in new ways. That's why, these days, I'm excited about filmmaking and the idea of highlighting activism through documentaries. In a lifetime of activism, I'm entering a new chapter, with new opportunities to try to make change that matters.

I hope you use some of these lessons to help you make change for the better. This book is about possibilities, not a blueprint. I hope the stories and examples I've shared here will inspire you to make a difference in your own way. We live in a time, more than ever, when successful activism is possible for almost everyone, with no initial need for resources or connections. This is, in a way, a revolutionary age of activism—when one person, with passion and persistence, can start a movement and ignite changes that can save lives, transform society, and maybe even save the world.

ACKNOWLEDGMENTS

I begin this book by describing it as a love letter to activism. I have dedicated my life to activism, and I have worked with so many people on the causes that mattered to me that any attempt to thank them all by name would run hundreds of pages long. I am indebted to all the people that have worked alongside me to help make a difference in our world our world. Successful activism takes a community, and I am proud of the communities that have included me among their ranks.

I would like to extend my deepest appreciation to the remarkable individuals who have influenced the creation of this book and are mentioned throughout it. To all those who have supported me in this enterprise, I extend my heartfelt thanks. Your presence has been a guiding light, and I am honored to have shared this experience with each and every one of you.

Many people shared my path in writing this book. Susan Wells and Larisa Kostov, your expertise and guidance have been instrumental in shaping the content of this book. Your meticulous research and organizational skills have brought clarity and coherence to this work. I am grateful for your assistance, your attention to detail, and your dedication to excellence.

Eva Avery and Erin Brown, your editorial process and keen eye for detail have helped polish this manuscript. Your commitment to excellence has elevated this work to new heights, and I thank you for your invaluable contributions.

To those who read the book in its earlier stages—Deborah Dunn, Jason Silverman, and Galia Granot—your insightful feedback and constructive criticism have played a pivotal role in shaping the narrative of this book. I am thankful for your dedication to the project and valuable contributions.

Dr. Hanna Shaul Bar Nissim, your collaboration and contributions have enriched the fabric of this book. Your insight and expertise have added depth and dimension to these pages, and I am thankful for your involvement.

I want to thank Octavia Spencer who wrote the foreword to this book. My life has been enriched through our friendship. I also want to express my gratitude to the following people for endorsing this book: Joseph Aoun, Northeastern University President; Congressman Tony Coelho; Geena Davis, actress; Bobby Farrelly, director; Peter Farrelly, director; Abe Foxman, National Director Emeritus of ADL; Senator Tom Harkin; Bill Kramer, CEO of the Academy of Motion Picture Arts and Sciences; Congressman Jim Langevin; Ron Liebowitz, Brandeis University President Emeritus; Julianna Margulies, actress; Marlee Matlin, actress; Norm Ornstein, Emeritus Scholar of the American Enterprise Institute; Tiffany

Smith Anoa'I, Executive Vice President of Entertainment, Diversity, Inclusion, and Communications at Paramount Global; and Judy Woodruff, former anchor of *PBS NewsHour*. You have all been invaluable partners in my activism journey.

I am grateful for the advice and backing of the board of the Ruderman Family Foundation, including one of the most humble and intelligent people I have ever known, Lon Jacobs. I also want to express my appreciation to all my colleagues who have worked with me at the foundation throughout the years.

Life is fuller when you have the support of good friends. I am grateful for the constant conversations I have with Dan Ocko, Rabbi Yossi Lipsker, and Derrek Shulman. You have always lifted my spirits when I have faced challenges.

The love and guidance that my wife, Shira, has provided me since we met has made me a better person. She has been my partner in life, and any successes I have had in life are due in large part to her sage advice. I'm lucky to have four amazing children. Michael, Tamar, Yehonatan, and Ariel, I'm so proud of you, and I'm lucky that you came into my life.

I am indebted to my sister, Sharon, who has been both a partner and friend. The encouragement and support of my parents, Morton z"l and Marcia, and brother, Todd, have been a bedrock in my life. You have propelled me forward, and I am appreciative that you have always been there for me.

Finally, thank you to all who will read this book. I hope you find it valuable as you forge your path to find your fight and improve our world.

NOTES

INTRODUCTION

1. Lynn Elber, "NBCUniversal Vows Auditions for Actors with Disabilities," *Associated Press*, January 29, 2021, https://apnews.com/article/technology-entertainment-a94d133c11d45d048970816f92e1667b; Rebecca Sun, "CBS Signs Pledge to Audition Actors with Disabilities," *Hollywood Reporter*, June 19, 2019, https://www.hollywoodreporter.com/tv/tv-news/cbs-signs-pledge-audition-actors-disabilities-1219640/; Greg Evans, "NBCUniversal Adopts Guidelines to Audition Actors with Disabilities," *Deadline*, January 29, 2021, https://deadline.com/2021/01/nbc-disabilities-auditions-guidelines-ruderman-family-foundation-1234683678/; Antonio Ferme, "Paramount Commits to Auditioning Actors with Disabilities," *Variety*, May 3, 2021, https://variety.com/2021/film/news/paramount-pictures-audition-disabilities-ruderman-family-foundation-1234965517/; David Robb, "Sony Pictures Entertainment Signs Ruderman Family Foundation Pledge to Audition Actors with Disabilities on Every New Show," *Deadline*, September 3, 2021, https://deadline.com/2021/09/sony-to-audition-actors-with-disabilities-on-every-new-show-ruderman-family-foundation-1234827115/.

2. Renata S. Geraldo, "Film Academy Turns Attention to Actors with Disabilities," *Bloomberg*, June 22, 2020, https://www.bloomberg.com/news/articles/2020-06-22/film-academy-s-diversity-push-turns-to-actors-with-disabilities?embedded-checkout=true.

3. Victor Mather, "The 'Disabled List' in Baseball Gets Deactivated," *New York Times*, February 8, 2019, https://www.nytimes.com/2019/02/08/sports/disabled-list-baseball.html.

4. Melissa Gray and Samuel Roth, "United Airlines Apologizes after Disabled Man Crawls off Flight," *CNN*, October 27, 2015, https://www.cnn.com/2015/10/25/us/united-airlines-disabled-man/index.html; Michael E. Miller, "D'Arcee

Neal: Disabled Activist Who Had to Crawl off United Airlines Flight Reveals the Humiliation That Followed," *Independent*, October 28, 2015, https://www.independent.co.uk/news/world/americas/the-disabled-gay-activist-who-had-to-crawl-off-his-united-airlines-flight-and-into-even-more-humiliation-a6711626.html.

CHAPTER 1

1. Reggie Ugwu, "The Hashtag That Changed the Oscars: An Oral History," *New York Times*, September 9, 2020, https://www.nytimes.com/2020/02/06/movies/oscarssowhite-history.html; Michael Wittner, "Ruderman Foundation Helps Secure Equal Pay for Paralympians, " *Jewish Journal*, October 4, 2018, https://jewishjournal.org/2018/10/04/ruderman-foundation-helps-secure-equal-pay-for-Paralympians/.

2. Jim Donnelly, "Watch Ellen DeGeneres' Coming Out Episode of Ellen Free Online!" *ABC*, April 28, 2017, https://abc.com/news/insider/watch-ellen-the-puppy-episode-free-for-its-20th-anniversary-celebration-041917.

3. Ruderman Family Foundation, "Open Letter to the Entertainment Industry," January 27, 2020, https://rudermanfoundation.org/press_releases/open-letter-to-the-entertainment-industry/; David Robb, "Stars Call on Hollywood to Increase Casting of Actors with Disabilities," *Deadline*, December 20, 2019, https://deadline.com/2019/12/hollywood-open-letter-increase-casting-of-actors-with-disabilities-1202815148/.

4. Chrissy Beckles, interview with Jay Ruderman, "Chrissy Beckles—Giving New Life to Stray Dogs in Puerto Rico," *All About Change*, podcast audio, December 11, 2023, https://rudermanfoundation.org/podcasts/chrissy-beckles-giving-new-life-to-stray-dogs-in-puerto-rico/; Chrissy Beckles, interview with Elizabeth Novogratz, "Chrissy Beckles: Golden Gloves Boxer in the Fight of Her Life," *Species Unite*, podcast audio, May 30, 2023, https://www.speciesunite.com/podcast/chrissy-beckles; Robin Finn, "Operation Paws," *New York Times*, March 24, 2012, https://www.nytimes.com/2012/03/25/nyregion/christina-beckles-boxer-and-dog-rescuer.html; "Checking in with Sato Project Founder Chrissy Beckles," *Moroccanoil*, March 8, 2022, https://www.moroccanoil.com/blogs/blog/checking-in-with-sato-project-founder-chrissy-beckles.

5. Lynn Smith, "MADD at 20: Still a Force for Change," *Los Angeles Times*, April 2, 2000, https://www.latimes.com/archives/la-xpm-2000-apr-02-cl-15045-story.html.

6. "Statistics," *MADD*, https://madd.org/statistics/.

7. Smith, "MADD at 20."

8. Smith, "MADD at 20."

9. Elizabeth Williamson, "Here's What Jones Has Said about Sandy Hook," *New York Times*, September 22, 2022, https://www.nytimes.com/2022/09/22/us/politics/heres-what-jones-has-said-about-sandy-hook.html.
10. "Safer Schools through Proven Prevention Programs," *Sandy Hook Promise*, https://www.sandyhookpromise.org/our-programs/program-overview/.
11. Amna Nawaz and Dorothy Hastings, "Jury orders conspiracy theorist Alex Jones to pay Sandy Hook families nearly $1 billion," PBS News, Oct 12, 2022, https://www.pbs.org/newshour/show/jury-orders-conspiracy-theorist-alex-jones-to-pay-sandy-hook-families-nearly-1-billion.
12. Nicole Hockley, interview with Jay Ruderman, "Losing a Child to Gun Violence—Nicole Hockley," *All Inclusive with Jay Ruderman*, podcast audio, May 23, 2022, https://allinclusivepodcast.com/podcasts/losing-a-child-to-americas-gun-violence-nicole-hockley/; Sandy Hook Promise, https://www.sandyhookpromise.org/; Chris Canipe and Travis Hartman, "A Timeline of Mass Shootings in the U.S.," *Reuters*, May 31, 2021, https://graphics.reuters.com/USA-GUNS/MASS-SHOOTING/nmovardgrpa/.

CHAPTER 2

1. Oxford Reference, "Calvin Coolidge 1872–1933," https://www.oxfordreference.com/view/10.1093/acref/9780191826719.001.0001/q-oro-ed4-00003260.
2. Chrissy Beckles, interview with Jay Ruderman, "Chrissy Beckles—Giving New Life to Stray Dogs in Puerto Rico," *All About Change*, podcast audio, December 11, 2023, https://rudermanfoundation.org/podcasts/chrissy-beckles-giving-newlife-to-stray-dogs-in-puerto-rico/.
3. Brenda Jones, interview with Jay Ruderman, "Civil Rights Leader John Lewis and the Power of Non-Violence with Brenda Jones," *All Inclusive with Jay Ruderman*, podcast audio, March 15, 2021, https://podscripts.co/podcasts/all-about-change/civil-rights-leader-john-lewis-and-the-power-of-non-violence-with-brenda-jones; Rashawn Ray, "Five Things John Lewis Taught Us about Getting in 'Good Trouble,'" *Brookings*, July 23, 2020, https://www.brookings.edu/articles/five-things-john-lewis-taught-us-about-getting-in-good-trouble/; Amy Klobuchar, "Statement on the Passing of Representative John Lewis," *Medium*, July 18, 2020, https://medium.com/@Amy_Klobuchar/statement-on-the-passing-of-representative-john-lewis-5f44b4299fea.
4. Wikipedia, "Lifestyles of the Rich and Famous," https://en.wikipedia.org/wiki/Lifestyles_of_the_Rich_and_Famous; "The Year of the Yuppies," *New York Times*, March 25, 1984, https://www.nytimes.com/1984/03/25/opinion/the-year-of-the-yuppies.html; Garry Trudeau, "Newsweek–Year of the Yuppie," *Artwork Archive*,

1984, https://www.artworkarchive.com/profile/the-doonesbury-collector/artwork/newsweek-year-of- the-yuppie.

5. Adam Burnstein, "Ruth S. Morgenthau, 75; Expert on Aid to Africa," *Washington Post*, November 16, 2006, https://www.washingtonpost.com/archive/local/2006/11/17/ruth-s-morgenthau-75/e7531e5c-430e-47ef-9a42-7b395f604cf6/.

6. Richard A. Hogarty, "The Harringtons of Salem: A Study of Massachusetts Politics," *New England Journal of Public Policy* 16: no. 1 (2000), https://scholarworks.umb.edu/nejpp/vol16/iss1/6/; "Mayors of Salem," *City of Salem*, https://www.salem.com/mayors-office/pages/mayors-salem.

7. Gloria Feldt, interview with Jay Ruderman, "Gloria Feldt—Feminist Icon," *All About Change*, podcast audio, October 24, 2022, https://rudermanfoundation.org/podcasts/gloria-feldt-feminist-icon/; "An Interview with Gloria Feldt: Talking Sanger, Fame, and the First Woman President," *Margaret Sanger Papers Project*, Research Annex, October 17, 2012, https://sangerpapers.wordpress.com/2012/10/17/an-interview-with-gloria-feldt-talking-sanger-fame-and-the-first-woman-president/.

8. Steve Beynon, "VA Has Denied about 78% of Disability Claims from Burn Pits," *Stars and Stripes*, September 23, 2020, https://www.stripes.com/veterans/va-has-denied-about-78-of-disability-claims-from-burn-pits-1.646181.

9. Kate Sullivan, "Biden Signs Bill Expanding Health Care Benefits for Veterans Exposed to Toxic Burn Pits," *CNN*, August 11, 2022, https://www.cnn.com/2022/08/10/politics/biden-burn-pits-bill-signing/index.html.

10. Le Roy Torres, interview with Jay Ruderman, "Veterans Speak out on the Dangers of Burn Pits," *All About Change*, podcast audio, October 30, 2023, https://rudermanfoundation.org/podcasts/le-roy-torres-veterans-speak-out-on-the-dangers-of-burn-pits; Michael McAuliff, "How a Texas Couple Led a Long Crusade and Won Protections for Veterans Exposed to Toxic Fumes," *Kaiser Health News*, August 8, 2022, https://www.texastribune.org/2022/08/08/texas-burn-pit-bill/; Crystal Dominguez, "Decade-Long Fight Ends with Burn Pit Victim Benefits," *Spectrum News 1*, June 23, 2022, https://spectrumlocalnews.com/tx/south-texas-el-paso/news/2022/06/23/burn-pit-pact-act.

CHAPTER 3

1. Danny Woodburn and Kristina Kopić, Ruderman Family Foundation, "Employment of Actors with Disabilities in Television, 2016," July 2016, https://rudermanfoundation.org/white_papers/employment-of-actors-with-disabilities-in-television/.

2. "CDC: 1 in 4 US adults live with a disability," *CDC Newsroom*, August 16, 2018, https://www.cdc.gov/media/releases/2018/p0816-disability.html.

3. David Robb, "Sony Pictures Entertainment Signs Ruderman Family Foundation Pledge to Audition Actors with Disabilities on Every New Show," *Deadline*, September 3, 2021, https://deadline.com/2021/09/sony-to-audition-actors-with-disabilities-on-every-new-show-ruderman-familyfoundation-1234827115/.

4. Ashley Roberts, "The School to Prison Pipeline," The Dyslexia Initiative, October 2, 2020, https://www.thedyslexiainitiative.org/post/the-school-to-prison-pipeline.

5. Hanna Shaul Bar Nissim, PhD, Ruderman Family Foundation, "Disability Inclusion in Movies and Television Market Research, 2019," white paper, September 13, 2019, https://rudermanfoundation.org/white_papers/disability-inclusion-in-movies-and-television-market-research-2019/; Ruderman Family Foundation, "Ruderman White Paper Reveals: Students with Disabilities Are Almost Twice as Likely to Be Victims of Cyberbullying," white paper, June 25, 2019, https://rudermanfoundation.org/white_papers/ruderman-white-paper-reveals-students-with-disabilities-are-almost-twice-as-likely-to-be-victims-of-cyberbullying/.

6. Wulf Rössler, "The Stigma of Mental Disorders: A Millennia-Long History of Social Exclusion and Prejudices," *EMBO Reports* 17, no. 9 (September 2016): 1250–1253, https://doi.org/10.15252%2Fembr.201643041.

7. National Institute of Mental Health, https://www.nimh.nih.gov/health/statistics/suicide.

8. American College Health Association, "National College Health Assessment II: Reference Group Executive Summary," Spring 2019, https://www.acha.org/documents/ncha/NCHA-II_SPRING_2019_US_REFERENCE_GROUP_EXECUTIVE_SUMMARY.pdf.

9. Miriam Heyman, PhD, Ruderman Family Foundation, "Ivy League Schools Fail Students with Mental Illness, 2018," December 10, 2018, https://rudermanfoundation.org/white_papers/the-ruderman-white-paper-reveals-ivy-league-schools-fail-students-with-mental-illness/#:~:text=Based%20on%20the%20report's%20analysis,Cornell%20University%20(D%2D)%2C%20Dartmouth.

10. Ruderman Family Foundation, "The Ruderman White Paper Reveals: Ivy League Schools Fail Students with Mental Illness," white paper, December 10, 2018, https://rudermanfoundation.org/white_papers/the-ruderman-white-paper-reveals-ivy-league-schools-fail-students-with-mental-illness/; Dori S. Hutchinson and Sharon Shapiro, "COVID-19 Creates Framework for Permanent Campus Culture That Supports Mental Health," *Diverse: Issues in Higher Education*, February 5, 2021, https://www.diverseeducation.com/covid- 19/article/15108613/covid-19-creates-framework-for-permanent-campus-culture-that-supports-mental-health; Stephanie Gilbert, "The Importance of Community and Mental Health," *National Alliance on Mental Illness (NAMI)*, November 18, 2019, https://www.nami.org/Blogs/NAMI-Blog/November-2019/The-Importance-of- Community-and-Mental-Health;

Ruderman Family Foundation, "Mental Health," https://rudermanfoundation. org/mental-health/; United States Department of Justice, "Justice Department Reaches Agreement with Brown University to Ensure Equal Access for Students with Mental Health Disabilities," press release, August 10, 2021, https://www.justice. gov/opa/pr/justice-department-reaches-agreement-brown-university-ensure-equal-access-students-mental; Rich Barlow, "BU Co-Creates First-of-Its-Kind Guides for Students Seeking a Mental Health Leave, and for Faculty and Staff," *BU Today*, April 27, 2021, https://www.bu.edu/articles/2021/bu-creates-guides-for-students-faculty-staff-seeking-a-mental-health-leave/; Jack Walker and Caelyn Pender, "Brown Reaches Settlement with U.S. Department of Justice after Wrongly Denying Readmission to Students on Mental Health Medical Leave," *Brown Daily Herald*, August 11, 2021, https://www.browndailyherald.com/2021/08/11/brown-reaches-settlement-u-s-department-justice-wrongly-denying-readmission-students-mental-health-medical-leave/.

11. Miriam Heyman, Jeff Dill, and Robert Douglass, "The Ruderman White Paper on Mental Health and Suicide of First Responders," Ruderman Family Foundation, April 2018, https://dir.nv.gov/uploadedFiles/dirnvgov/content/WCS/TrainingDocs/First%20Responder%20White%20Paper_Final%20(2).pdf.

12. Heyman, Dill, and Douglass, "The Ruderman White Paper on Mental Health and Suicide of First Responders," "Rosen, Fischer Re-Introduce Bipartisan Bill to Address Firefighter, First Responder Mental Health," *Jacky Rosen, U.S. Senator for Nevada* (Official Website), August 18, 2021, https://www.rosen.senate.gov/rosen-fischer-re-introduce-bipartisan-bill-address-firefighter-first-responder-mental-health; Suicide Prevention Resource Center, "First Responders," https://www.sprc.org/settings/first- responders.

13. Geena Davis, interview with Jay Ruderman, "Geena Davis—Dying of Politeness," *All About Change*, podcast audio, January 3, 2023, https://rudermanfoundation. org/podcasts/geena-davis-dying-of-politeness/; "About Us," *Geena Davis Institute on Gender in Media*, https://seejane.org/about-us/.

14. Kevin Love, interview with Jay Ruderman, "Kevin Love—Professional Basketball Star, Mental Health Advocate, & Founder of the Kevin Love Fund," *All Inclusive with Jay Ruderman*, podcast audio, March 15, 2021, https://allinclusivepodcast. com/podcasts/kevin-love-professional-basketball-star-mental-health-advocate-founder-of-the-kevin-love-fund/; "Changing the Conversation around Mental Health: An Interview with Kevin Love, Professional Basketball Player, Mental Health Advocate, and Founder, Kevin Love Fund," *Leaders*, October 4, 2022, https://www.leadersmag.com/issues/2022.4_Oct/PDFs/LEADERS-Kevin-Love-Kevin-Love-Fund.pdf.

15. Emily Penn, interview with Jay Ruderman, "Emily Penn—Microplastics, Ocean Pollution, and Female Health," *All About Change*, podcast audio,

September 4, 2023, https://rudermanfoundation.org/podcasts/emily-penn-microplastics-ocean-pollution-and-female-health/; Elizabeth Oliver, "At the Moment, I'm Optimistic about the Future of Our Ocean," *Making Waves*, Royal Museum Greenwich, https://www.rmg.co.uk/stories/topics/making-waves/emily-penn; Katie Strick, "World Oceans Day: Sailor Emily Penn on Why Plastic Pollution Is a Women's Issue," *The Standard*, March 8, 2021, https://www.standard.co.uk/lifestyle/sailor-emily-penn-plastic-pollution-world-oceans-day-b922906.html; Nirandhi Gowthaman, "Architect Turned Environmentalist Emily Penn Leads an All-Woman Voyage to Tackle Plastic Pollution," *Herstory*, February 17, 2020, https://yourstory.com/herstory/2020/02/architect-environmentalist-women-voyage-globe.

16. Lawrence Bacow, interview with Jay Ruderman, "President of Harvard University, Lawrence Bacow," *All Inclusive with Jay Ruderman*, podcast audio, August 17, 2020, https://rudermanfoundation.org/podcast/season-3-episode-10-president-of-harvard-lawrence-bacow-on-covid-19-mental-health-and-racial-injustice-in-society/.

17. Serge Kovaleski, "Obama's Organizing Years, Guiding Others and Finding Himself," *New York Times*, July 7, 2008, https://www.nytimes.com/2008/07/07/us/politics/07community.html; Jodi Kantor, "In Law School, Obama Found Political Voice," *New York Times*, January 28, 2007, https://www.nytimes.com/2007/01/28/us/politics/28obama.html; Lisa Philip, "Obama Shares Words of Advice with a New Generation of Community Organizers," *Chicago Sun-Times*, May 10, 2023, https://chicago.suntimes.com/education/2023/5/10/23719198/obama-shares-words-of-advice-with-a-new-generation-of-community-organizers; David Moberg, "Obama's Community Roots," *The Nation*, April 3, 2007, https://www.thenation.com/article/archive/obamas-community-roots/; Maurice Possley, "Activism Blossomed in College," *Chicago Tribune*, March 30, 2007, https://www.chicagotribune.com/2007/03/30/activism-blossomed-in-college-2; Ryan Lizza, "The Agitator," *New Republic*, March 18, 2007, https://newrepublic.com/article/64660/the-agitator.

CHAPTER 4

1. Jeff Passan, "Major League Baseball to rename disabled list as 'injured list,'" ESPN, February 7, 2019, https://www.espn.com/mlb/story/_/id/25947020/major-league-baseball-rename-disabled-list-injured-list.

2. Michael Wittner, "Ruderman Foundation Helps Secure Equal Pay for Paralympians," *Jewish Journal*, October 4, 2018, https://jewishjournal.org/2018/10/04/ruderman-foundation-helps-secure-equal-pay-for-Paralympians.

3. Arutz Sheva Staff, "Israel to invest in accessible intercity buses," Israel National News, August 4, 2012, https://www.israelnationalnews.com/news/311143.

4. "About Our History," NAACP, accessed July 23, 2024, https://naacp.org/about/our-history#:~:text=The%20New%20Millennium,presidential%20election%20than%20in%201996.

5. Natasha Abhayawickrama, "Climate Activism Isn't Making Young People Anxious. Climate Change Is," *The Guardian*, September 3, 2021, https://www.theguardian.com/commentisfree/2021/sep/04/climate-activism-isnt-making-young-people-anxious-climate-change-is.

6. Juliet Grable, "A New Hope for Shutting Down the Dakota Access Pipeline," *Sierra*, November 14, 2023, https://www.sierraclub.org/sierra/new-hope-shutting-down-dakota-access-pipeline; Justin Worland, "What To Know about the Dakota Access Pipeline Protests," *Time*, October 28, 2016, https://time.com/4548566/dakota-access-pipeline-standing-rock-sioux/; Leah Donnella, "At the Sacred Stone Camp, Tribes and Activists Join Forces to Protect the Land," *NPR*, September 10, 2016, https://www.npr.org/sections/codeswitch/2016/09/10/493110892/at-the-sacred-stone-camp-a-coalition-joins-forces-to-protect-the-land; Kristen A. Carpenter and Angela R. Riley, "Standing Tall," *Slate*, September 23, 2016, https://slate.com/news-and-politics/2016/09/why-the-sioux-battle-against-the-dakota-access-pipeline-is-such-a-big-deal.html; "Dakota Access: Stars from Hollywood to Washington Support Water Protesters," *Indian Country Today*, September 13, 2018, https://ictnews.org/archive/dakota-access-stars-from-hollywood-to-washington-support-water-protectors; Valerie Volcovici, "Sanders, 4 Other Senators Request Pipeline Review as 19 Cities Support Tribe," *Grand Forks Herald*, October 13, 2016, https://www.grandforksherald.com/news/sanders-4-other-senators-request-dakota-pipeline-review-as-19-cities-support-tribe; Derek Gentile, "Great Barrington Chef Cooks Thanksgiving Dinner at Standing Rock," *Berkshire Eagle*, November 22, 2016, https://web.archive.org/web/20161128133527/http://www.berkshireeagle.com/stories/great-barrington-chef-cooks-thanksgiving-dinner-at-standing-rock,490194; Jeff Gammage, "Philly Restaurateurs to Serve Thanksgiving Dinner at Standing Rock," *Philadelphia Inquirer*, November 28, 2016, https://www.inquirer.com/philly/news/20161124_Philly_pilgrims_travel_west_to_serve_Thanksgiving_dinner_to_Indians.html; Daniel A. Medina and Chiara Sottile, "Scores Arrested in Dakota Access Protests Nationwide," *NBC News*, November 22, 2016, https://www.nbcnews.com/storyline/dakota-pipeline-protests/scores-arrested-dakota-access-pipeline-protests-nationwide-n684531; Christopher Mele, "Veterans to Serve as 'Human Shields' for Dakota Pipeline Protesters," *New York Times*, November 29, 2016, https://www.nytimes.com/2016/11/29/us/veterans-to-serve-as-human-shields-for-pipeline-protesters.html; Stephanie R. Januchowski-Hartley, Ann Hillborn, Katherine C. Crocker, and Asia Murphy, "Scientists Stand with Standing Rock," *Science*, September 30, 2016, https://www.science.org/doi/10.1126/science.aaj2057; Nayanika Guha, "6 Years after Standing Rock, Native Tribes Still Fight Dakota Access Pipeline," *Truthout*, October 9, 2023, https://truthout.org/articles/5-years-after-standing-rock-native-tribes-still-fight-dakota-access-pipeline/.

7. "VA Research Reveals Circumstances That Can Lead to Homelessness among Women Veterans," *VA News*, March 31, 2020, https://news.va.gov/73113/va-research-reveals-circumstances-can-lead-homelessness-women-veterans/.

8. "Veteran Homeless Facts," *Green Doors*, https://greendoors.org/facts/veteran-homelessness.php.

9. "Homeless Women Veterans: Actions Needed to Ensure Safe and Appropriate Housing," *U.S. Government Accountability Office*, December 23, 2011, https://www.gao.gov/products/gao-12-182.

10. Jas Boothe, interview with Jay Ruderman, "Jas Boothe—Standing Up for Female Veterans," *All About Change*, podcast audio, October 2, 2023, https://rudermanfoundation.org/podcasts/jas-boothe-standing-up-for-female-veterans/; "Jas Boothe, American Dream U Advisor," *American Dream U*, https://americandreamu.org/jas-boothe/.

11. Kevin Hines, interview with Jay Ruderman, "Kevin Hines—Surviving and Thriving," *All About Change*, podcast audio, October 3, 2022, https://rudermanfoundation.org/podcasts/kevin-hines-surviving-thriving/; Tad Friend, "Jumpers: The Fatal Grandeur of the Golden Gate Bridge," *New Yorker*, October 5, 2003, https://www.newyorker.com/magazine/2003/10/13/jumpers; Remy Melina, "How Did Teen Survive Fall from Golden Gate Bridge?," *Live Science*, April 19, 2022, https://www.livescience.com/33221-teen-survives-fall-from-golden-gate-bridge.html; Mike Weiss, "Lethal Beauty/A Survivor's Story: A Jumper Advocates for a Barrier and Makes a New Life," *SFGate*, November 1, 2005, https://www.sfgate.com/news/article/Lethal-Beauty-A-Survivor-s-Story-A-jumper-2598731.php; Bridge Rail Foundation, http://www.bridgerail.net/; Rachel Swan, "Golden Gate Bridge Suicide Nets Delayed Two Years, as People Keep Jumping," *San Francisco Chronicle*, December 12, 2019, https://www.sfchronicle.com/bayarea/article/Golden-Gate-Bridge-suicide-nets- delayed-two-14900278.php.

CHAPTER 5

1. Joshua Bote, "'Get in Good Trouble, Necessary Trouble': Rep. John Lewis in His Own Words," *USA Today*, July 19, 2020, https://www.usatoday.com/story/news/politics/2020/07/18/rep-john-lewis-most-memorable-quotes-get-good-trouble/5464148002/.

2. Michael Specter, "How Act Up Changed America," *New Yorker*, June 7, 2021, https://www.newyorker.com/magazine/2021/06/14/how-act-up-changed-america.

3. Nurith Aizenman, "How to Demand a Medical Breakthrough: Lessons from the AIDS Fight," *NPR Health News*, February 9, 2019, https://www.npr.org/sections/health-shots/2019/02/09/689924838/how-to-demand-a-medical-breakthrough-lessons-from-the-aids-fight.

4. Tarana Burke, "I Founded 'Me Too' in 2006. The Morning It Went Viral Was a Nightmare," *Time,* September 14, 2021, https://time.com/6097392/tarana-burke-me-too-unbound-excerpt/

5. Burke, "I Founded 'Me Too.'"

6. Abby Ohlheiser, "The Woman behind 'Me Too' Knew the Power of the Phrase When She Created It—10 Years Ago," *Washington Post*, October 19, 2017, https://www.washingtonpost.com/news/the-intersect/wp/2017/10/19/the-woman-behind-me-too-knew-the-power-of-the-phrase-when-she-created-it-10-years-ago.

7. Sopan Deb, "Donald Trump Mocks Reporter's Disability," *CBS News*, November 25, 2015, https://www.cbsnews.com/news/donald-trump-mocks-reporters-disability/.

8. Daniel Arkin, "Donald Trump Criticized after He Appears to Mock Reporter Serge Kovaleski," *NBC News*, November 26, 2015, https://www.nbcnews.com/politics/2016-election/donald-trump-criticized-after-he-appears-mock-reporter-serge-kovaleski-n470016; Callum Borchers, "People Love It When Donald Trump Makes Fun of Journalists—except One in Particular," *Washington Post*, August 10, 2016, https://www.washingtonpost.com/news/the-fix/wp/2016/08/10/people-love-it-when-donald-trump-makes-fun-of-journalists-except-one-in-particular/; "Group Offers Sensitivity Training to Trump after He Appears to Mock Reporter's Disability," *CBS New York*, November 26, 2015, https://www.cbsnews.com/newyork/news/donald-trump-sensitivity-training-offer/; Reuters, "Donald Trump Drops 12 Percentage Points in Week," *Voice of America*, November 28, 2015, https://www.voanews.com/usa/poll-trump-drops-12-percentage-points-week.

9. Joe Otterson, "50 Cent under Fire for Mocking Autistic Janitor at Cincinnati Airport (Video)," *The Wrap*, May 3, 2016, https://www.thewrap.com/50-cent-austistic-teen-cincinnati-airport-backlash-twitter-instagram-video/.

10. Andrea Park, "Rapper 50 Cent Mocked Autistic Man on Twitter," *CBS News*, May 3, 2016, https://www.cbsnews.com/news/rapper-50-cent-mocked-autistic-man-on-twitter/.

11. Travis Andrews, "Rapper 50 Cent Publicly Mocks Autistic Teen, Then Apologizes after Outraged Reaction," *Washington Post*, May 4, 2016, https://www.washingtonpost.com/news/morning-mix/wp/2016/05/04/rapper-50-cent-publicly-mocks-autistic-teen-then-apologizes-after-outraged-reaction/; Lola Ogunnaike, "50 Cent: Taking Care of Business—The Battle between 50 Cent and Kanye West Could Answer the Question: Who Is the King of Hip-Hop?," *Rolling Stone*, September 20, 2007, https://www.rollingstone.com/music/music-news/50-cent-taking-care-of-business-193669/; Brian Hamrick, "50 Cent Berates Disabled CVG Worker in Expletive-Laced Video," *WLWT*, May 3, 2016, https://www.wlwt.com/article/50-cent-berates-disabled-cvg-worker-in-expletive-laced-video/3565080#; "Family of

Autistic Man Mocked by 50 Cent Accepts Apology," *BBC News*, May 4, 2016, https://www.bbc.com/news/newsbeat-36202408; Adelle Platon, "50 Cent Apologizes for Mocking Autistic Airport Employee on Instagram," *Billboard Magazine*, May 4, 2016, https://www.billboard.com/articles/columns/hip-hop/7356856/50-cent-apology-autistic-airport-employee-andrew-farrell-instagram.

12. Haley Hunt, "Kylie Jenner Condemned for Posting Photo While Seemingly Parked in Disabled Spot," *NBC Washington*, July 23, 2019, https://www.nbcwashington.com/news/national-international/jenner-condemned-for-posting-photo-parked-in-handicapped-designated-spot/83805/; Aurelie Corinthios, "Disability Group Slams Kylie Jenner and Travis Scott for Seemingly Parking in Accessible Spot," *People*, July 23, 2019, https://people.com/tv/kylie-jenner-travis-scott-slammed-disability-accessible-parking/.

13. Jojo Moyes, *Me Before You* (New York: Penguin Books, 2013); Thea Sharrock, dir. *Me Before You*. Burbank, CA: Warner Bros. Pictures, 2016.

14. Ruderman Family Foundation, "Ruderman Family Foundation Outraged Over 'Me Before You' Portrayal of People with Disabilities," June 2, 2016, https://rudermanfoundation.org/ruderman-family-foundation-outraged-over-me-before-you- portrayal-of-people-with-disabilities/.

15. Michael Mailer, dir. *Blind*. Brooklyn, NY: Michael Mailer Films, 2016.

16. "Disability Organisation Slams 'Blind' for Casting Alec Baldwin," *Business Standard*, July 6, 2017, https://www.business-standard.com/article/pti-stories/disability-organisation-slams-blind-for-casting-alec-baldwin-117070600204_1.html; William Hughes, "Disability Advocates Are Mad at Alex Baldwin for Playing a Blind Writer," *AV Club*, July 6, 2017, https://www.avclub.com/disability-advocates-are-mad-at-alec-baldwin-for-playin- 1798263724.

17. Post Editorial Board, "The Post Stands Up for Alec Baldwin," *New York Post*, July 10, 2017, https://nypost.com/2017/07/10/the-post-stands-up-for-alec-baldwin/.

18. Michael Mailer, "'Blind' Director Addresses Backlash over Casting Alec Baldwin and Not Disabled Actor in Lead Role," *Deadline*, July 14, 2017, https://deadline.com/2017/07/blind-alec-baldwin-backlash-director-responds-michael-mailer-1202129011/.

19. Jay Ruderman, "'Blind' Movie: Ruderman Foundation Responds to Director Over Alec Baldwin Casting Flap," *Deadline*, July 18, 2017, https://deadline.com/2017/07/blind-movie-controversy-alec-baldwin-ruderman-foundation-responds-guest-column-1202130794/.

20. Box Office Mojo, "Dwayne Johnson Movie Box Office Results," https://www.boxofficemojo.com/name/nm0425005/.

21. Hilary Lewis, "Dwayne Johnson, 'Skyscraper' Director Talk Partnership and Neve Campbell's Strong Character," *Hollywood Reporter*, July

14, 2018, https://www.hollywoodreporter.com/movies/movie-news/
skyscraper-rock-amputee-prep-director-neve-campbell-character-1127160/.

22. Hanifah Rahman, "The Rock's New Movie Has Sparked a Debate about Disability
Representation In Hollywood," *BuzzFeed*, July 17, 2018, https://www.buzzfeed.
com/hanifahrahman/the-rocks-new-movie-has-people-talking-about-disability.

23. Rahman, "The Rock's New Movie."

24. "Poland's Twisted Holocaust Law: Law Criminalizes Anyone Who Claims Polish
State Was Involved in Nazi War Crimes," *Human Rights Watch*, February 10, 2018,
https://www.hrw.org/news/2018/02/10/polands-twisted-holocaust-law.

25. Rachel Donadio, "The Dark Consequences of Poland's New Holocaust Law,"
The Atlantic, February 8, 2018, https://www.theatlantic.com/international/
archive/2018/02/poland-holocaust-law/552842/.

26. Donadio, "The Dark Consequences."

27. "AJC Decries New Video on Poland," *AJC Global Voice*, February 21, 2018, https://
www.ajc.org/news/ajc-decries-new-video-on-poland.

28. Donadio, "The Dark Consequences"; Christian Davies, "Poland Makes Partial
U-turn on Holocaust Law after Israel Row," *The Guardian*, June 27, 2018, https://
www.theguardian.com/world/2018/jun/27/poland-partial-u-turn-controversial-
holocaust-law; Vanessa Gera, "U of O Holocaust Scholar Ordered to Apologize
in Polish Libel Case," *CBC News*, August 17, 2021, https://www.cbc.ca/news/
canada/ottawa/holocaust-scholar-polish-libel-case-1.5907633; "Ruderman
Foundation Pulls Video Criticizing Poland's Holocaust Law," *Jewish Telegraphic
Agency*, February 22, 2018, https://www.jta.org/2018/02/22/united-states/
ruderman-family-foundation-pulls-video-criticizing-polands-holocaust-law;
Josh Nathan-Kazis, "'Polish Holocaust' Video Yanked by Foundation amid
Outcry," *Forward*, February 21, 2018, https://forward.com/news/394956/
foundation-pulls-video-urging-us-to-sever-ties-to-poland-and-accused-poles/.

29. "Socrates as the 'Gadfly' of the State," *Online Library of Liberty*, quote, https://oll.
libertyfund.org/quote/socrates-as-the-gadfly-of-the-state-4thc-bc.

30. Tom Jacobs, "Social Pressure Can Change Minds, Even on Divisive Issues,"
Pacific Standard, May 21, 2018, https://psmag.com/news/social-pressure-can-
change-minds-even-on-divisive-issues; Julia Steinberger, "Individuals and
Social Pressure: How to Change the World," *Medium*, January 23, 2022, https://
jksteinberger.medium.com/individuals-and-social-pressure-how-to-change-the-
world-8304ada3bbca; Arthur Dobrin, "The Astonishing Power of Social Pressure,"
Psychology Today, April 14, 2014, https://www.psychologytoday.com/us/blog/
am-i-right/201404/the-astonishing-power-social-pressure.

31. Gina Kolata, "Study Finds Big Social Factor in Quitting Smoking," *New York Times*,
May 22, 2008, https://www.nytimes.com/2008/05/22/science/22smoke.html.

32. Ronit Amit and Michal Shmuel, "Impact Report—Israel Unlimited: The Partnership That Changed the Lives of People with Disabilities in Israel," *Israel Unlimited*, March 2021.

33. Gary Kamiya, "Powerful Forces Wanted Freeways All over SF. Here's How They Were Stopped," *San Francisco Chronicle*, October 4, 2019, https://www.sfchronicle.com/bayarea/article/Powerful-forces-wanted-freeways-all-over-SF-14492380.php#.

34. Chris McGreal, "Boycotts and Sanctions Helped Rid South Africa of Apartheid—Is Israel Next in Line?" *The Guardian*, May 23, 2021, https://www.theguardian.com/world/2021/may/23/israel-apartheid-boycotts-sanctions-south-africa.

35. Judy Woodruff, interview with Jay Ruderman, "Judy Woodruff Talks Journalism and Inclusion," *All Inclusive with Jay Ruderman*, podcast audio, July 5, 2020, https://rudermanfoundation.org/podcast/season-3-episode-6-judy-woodruff-talks-journalism-and-disability-inclusion/.

36. Gloria Steinem, *My Life on the Road* (New York: Penguin Random House, 2016).

37. Sarah Pruitt, "For Gloria Steinem, Learning Means Listening," *Phillips Exeter Academy*, April 25, 2021, https://www.exeter.edu/news/gloria-steinem-learning-means-listening.

CHAPTER 6

1. Danny Woodburn, "If You Don't Really Mean Inclusion—Shut the F%&# Up!," *Huffington Post*, February 3, 2017, https://www.huffpost.com/entry/if-you-dont-really-mean-i_b_9153008.

2. "Danny Woodburn," *IMDB*, https://www.imdb.com/name/nm0940173/.

3. Danny Woodburn, interview with Jay Ruderman, "Fighting for Authentic Representation in Hollywood," *All Inclusive with Jay Ruderman*, podcast audio,, 2019, https://rudermanfoundation.org/podcast/episode-10-fighting-for-authentic-representation-in-hollywood/.

4. Danny Woodburn and Kristina Kopic, "The Ruderman White Paper on Employment of Actors with Disabilities in Television," Ruderman Family Foundation, white paper, July 2016, https://www.rudermanfoundation.org/wp-content/uploads/2016/07/TV-White-Paper_final.final_.pdf.

5. Peter Farrelly and Bobby Farrelly, interview with Jay Ruderman, "Holiday Special Featuring Acclaimed Filmmakers Peter and Bobby Farrelly," *All Inclusive with Jay Ruderman*, podcast audio, December 14, 2020, https://allinclusivepodcast.com/podcasts/holiday-special-featuring-acclaimed-filmmakers-peter-and-bobby-farrelly-part-1/.

6. "101 Funniest Screenplays," *Writers Guild of America West*, https://www.wga.org/writers-room/101-best-lists/101-funniest-screenplays/list.

7. "Open Letter to the Entertainment Industry," Ruderman Family Foundation, https://rudermanfoundation.org/pledge/.

8. Ruderman Family Foundation, "Foundation Honors Actress Marlee Matlin with Morton E. Ruderman Award in Inclusion," February 22, 2017, https://rudermanfoundation.org/actress-marlee-matlin-honored-with-morton-e-ruderman-award-in-inclusion/; William J. Kole "'Green Book' Director Farrelly, Brother Get Disability Award," *AP News*, https://apnews.com/article/68cbcf80 47797fb406227f91a1b98e6f; Ruderman Family Foundation, "Farrelly Brothers Honored with Morton E. Ruderman Award for Inclusion of People with Disabilities," December 4, 2019, https://rudermanfoundation.org/press_releases/farrelly-brothers-honored-with-morton-e- ruderman-award-for-inclusion-of-people-with-disabilities/.

9. Genesis Butler, "A 10-Year-Old's Vision for Healing the Planet | TEDxCSULB," *YouTube*, May 19, 2017, https://www.youtube.com/watch?v=E4ptaIDAIlY.

10. Genesis Butler, interview with Jay Ruderman, "Genesis Butler—Amplifying Youth Activism," *All About Change*, podcast audio, July 23, 2023, https://rudermanfoundation.org/podcasts/genesis-butler-amplifying-youth-activism/; Via Ryerson, "8 Questions for Genesis Butler," *Time for Kids*, March 30, 2022, https://www.timeforkids.com/g56/g5-genesis-8q/.

11. Genesis Butler, interview with Jay Ruderman, *All About Change*.

12. Ruderman Family Foundation, *YouTube*, July 26, 2020, https://www.youtube.com/watch?v=RYcKlnIc63M.

13. Dino-Ray Ramos, "Octavia Spencer Teams with Ruderman Family Foundation to Demand More Authentic Casting of People with Disabilities in Film & TV," *Deadline*, July 27, 2020, https://deadline.com/2020/07/octavia-spencer-ruderman-family-foundation-casting-disabilities-film-tv-hollywood-1202996185/.

14. Kristen Lopez, "Why 'The Peanut Butter Falcon' Changes the Disabled Narrative & Scared Hollywood," *Forbes*, August 5, 2019, https://www.forbes.com/sites/kristenlopez/2019/08/05/why-the-peanut-butter-falcon-changes-the-disabled-narrative--scared-hollywood/?sh=2620acf03518.

CHAPTER 7

1. Stephanie Y. Evans, *Black Women's Yoga History: Memoirs of Inner Peace* (Albany: State University of New York Press, 2021), 213–218.

2. Lisa Rofel and Jeremy Tai, "A Conversation with Ericka Huggins," *Feminist Studies* 42, no. 1, Everyday Militarism (2016), 236–248; Ericka Huggins, "The Importance of Considering Spiritual Practice if We Want to Serve Humanity," *Ericka Huggins: The Official Website*, July 6, 2017, https://www.erickahuggins.com/spirituality-social-justice.

3. Frederic and Mary Ann Brussat, book review, "The Selected Works of Audre Lorde," *Spirituality & Practice*, https://www.spiritualityandpractice.com/book-reviews/view/28958/the-selected-works-of-audre-lorde; Lenora A. Houseworth, "The Radical History of Self-Care," *Teen Vogue*, January 14, 2021, https://www.teenvogue.com/story/the-radical-history-of-self-care; Aisha Harris, "A History of Self-Care," *Slate*, April 5, 2017, https://www.slate.com/articles/arts/culturebox/2017/04/the_history_of_self_care.html; Natasha Takyi-Micah, "Origins of Self-Care and Why Activists and Advocates Need to Practice It," *The Center for Community Solutions*, April 10, 2023, https://www.communitysolutions.com/origins-of-self-care-and-why-activists-and-advocates-need-to-practice-it/.

4. Tricia Hersey, "Rest Is Resistance," *The Cut*, October 6, 2022, https://www.thecut.com/2022/10/rest-is-resistance-manifesto-nap-ministry-book-excerpt.html.

5. Tiffany Shlain, *24/6: The Power of Unplugging One Day a Week* (New York: Gallery Books, 2019).

6. George Lakey, "When Activist Burnout Was a Problem 50 Years Ago, This Group Found a Solution," *Waging Nonviolence*, May 21, 2020, https://wagingnonviolence.org/2020/05/activist-burnout-50-years-ago-movement-for-a-new-society/.

7. Rae Alexandra, "The Dancer Who Helped Start the Black Panthers' Free Breakfast Program," *Rebel Girls from Bay Area History*, February 14, 2024, https://www.kqed.org/arts/13950520/ruth-beckford-dance-black-panthers-free-breakfast-program.

8. Alexandra, "The Dancer Who Helped Start the Black Panthers' Free Breakfast Program"; Brenda Payton, "Obituary: Ruth Beckford, Legendary Dancer, Choreographer," *East Bay Times*, May 9, 2019, https://www.eastbaytimes.com/2019/05/09/obituary-ruth-beckford-legendary-dancer-choreographer/; "Why Self-Care and Collective Care Are Critical to Winning Change," *Moblab*, June 5, 2018, https://mobilisationlab.org/stories/moblab-live-self-care-collective-wellbeing/; Rushdia Mehreen and David Gray-Donald, "Be Careful with Each Other," *Briarpatch Magazine*, August 29, 2018, https://briarpatchmagazine.com/articles/view/be-careful-with-each-other.

9. Lori Michau and Sophie Namy, "Creating an Organizational Culture for Social Justice Activism," *Learning from Practice Series No. 1: Organizational Perspectives*, Raising Voices, https://raisingvoices.org/wp-content/uploads/2022/01/LP1.OrgCulture.FINALredesign.dec2015.pdf.

10. Katie Becker, "9 Activists Share Self Care Tips," *Teen Vogue*, June 19, 2017, https://www.teenvogue.com/gallery/nine-activist-self-care-tips; Michau

and Namy, "Creating an Organizational Culture"; Wangechi Wachira, Natsnet Ghebrebrhan, and Lori Michau, "Integrating Self-Care into VAW Programming and Organizations," *Raising Voices,* https://www.svri.org/forums/forum2019/Presentations/Integrating%20Self%20Care%20into%20VAW%20Programming%20and%20Organizations.pdf.

CHAPTER 8

1. Juliet Macur, "Simone Biles Is Withdrawing from the Olympic All-Around Gymnastics Competition," *New York Times,* July 28, 2021, https://www.nytimes.com/2021/07/28/sports/olympics/simone-biles-out.html; Bill Chappell, "Read What Simone Biles Said after Her Withdrawal from the Olympic Final," *NPR,* July 28, 2021, https://www.npr.org/sections/tokyo-olympics-live-updates/2021/07/28/1021683296/in-her-words-what-simone-biles-said-after-her-withdrawal; Louise Radnofsky and Andrew Beaton, "Simone Biles Plans a Return to Gymnastics Competition," *Wall Street Journal,* June 28, 2023, https://www.wsj.com/sports/olympics/simone-biles-paris-olympics-comeback-3493e4fa; "Biles Grateful for Support during 'Mental Health Journey,'" *Reuters,* October 11, 2023, https://www.reuters.com/sports/athletics/biles-grateful-support-during-mental-health-journey-2023-10-12; Sara Tardiff, "Simone Biles Called Dropping Out of the Tokyo Olympics Her 'Biggest Win,'" *Teen Vogue,* April 14, 2022, https://www.teenvogue.com/story/simone-biles-called-dropping-out-of-the-tokyo-olympics-her-biggest-win; Stephanie Apstein, "Simone Biles's Big 2023 Return Has Set Her Up for an Even Bigger Future," *Sports Illustrated,* December 27, 2023, https://www.si.com/olympics/2023/12/27/simone-biles-2023-return-has-set-her-up-for-paris-2024; Kurt Streeter, "Simone Biles and the Power of 'No,'" *New York Times,* July 28, 2021, https://www.nytimes.com/2021/07/28/sports/simone-biles-self-care.html.

2. Will Thorne, "Variety to Host Conference on Diversity and Inclusion in Hollywood," *Variety,* September 26, 2016, https://variety.com/2016/biz/news/variety-inclusion-conference-pharrell-williams-donna-langley-1201870256/.

3. Dave Zirin, "June 20, 1967: Muhammad Ali Convicted for Refusing the Vietnam Draft," *Zinn Education Project,* https://www.zinnedproject.org/news/tdih/-muhammad-ali-convicted-refusing-vietnam-draft.

4. Thomas Hauser, *Muhammad Ali: His Life and Times* (New York: Simon and Schuster, 1991).

5. Zirin, "June 20, 1967"; Audre Lorde, "The Transformation," *Genius,* https://genius.com/Audre-lorde-the-transformation-annotated.

CHAPTER 9

1. Nuseir Yassin, interview with Jay Ruderman, "Nas Daily and Bringing His Life from Good to Great," *All About Change*, podcast audio, January 28, 2024, https://allaboutchangepodcast.com/podcast-episode/8928; Eshita Bhargava, "NAS Daily Wants to Leave a Positive Mark on the World: International Vlogger Nuseir Yassin," *Outlook India*, December 14, 2020, https://www.outlookindia.com/art-entertainment/entertainment-news-nas-daily-wants-to-leave-a-positive-mark-on-the-world-international-vlogger-nuseir-yassin-news-367129.

2. "U.S. Supreme Court Takes Away the Constitutional Right to Abortion," Center for Reproductive Rights, https://reproductiverights.org/case/scotus-mississippi-abortion-ban/.

3. Sarita Gupta and Silvia Henriquez, "In the Wake of Roe, a Resurgent Fight for Reproductive Justice," *Ford Foundation*, January 2023, https://www.fordfoundation.org/news-and-stories/stories/in-the-wake-of-roe-a-resurgent-fight-for-reproductive-justice/; "What It's Like to Fight for Abortion Rights, Post-Roe," *ACLU*, January 30, 2023, https://www.aclu.org/news/reproductive-freedom/what-its-like-to-fight-for-abortion-rights-post-roe; Eleanor J. Bader, "'We Are in Survival Mode': How the End of Roe v. Wade Changed Abortion Activism," *The Progressive Magazine*, January 22, 2024, https://progressive.org/latest/how-the-end-of-roe-v-wade-changed-abortion-activism-bader-20240122/.

4. Hayleigh Evans, "Arizona Environmental Activists Say There's Too Much at Stake to Stop Their Fight," *Arizona Republic*, December 26, 2023, https://www.azcentral.com/story/news/local/arizona-environment/2023/12/26/arizona-climate-activists-plan-to-keep-fighting-for-action/71805798007.

5. Paul King, dir., *Wonka*, Burbank, CA: Warner Bros. Studios, 2023.

6. "Flint Water Crisis: Everything You Need to Know," *NRDC*, April 16, 2024, https://www.nrdc.org/stories/flint-water-crisis-everything-you-need-know.

7. Sara Ganim, "Flint Water Crisis Likely the Cause of Deadly Legionnaires Outbreak," *CNN*, March 30, 2017, https://www.cnn.com/2017/03/30/health/legionnaires-disease-flint-water-crisis-study/index.html.

8. Ken Meyer, "Asked and Answered: President Obama Responds to an Eight-Year-Old Girl from Flint." *The White House*, April 27, 2016, https://obamawhitehouse.archives.gov/blog/2016/04/27/asked-and-answered-president-obama-responds-eight-year-old-girl-flint.

9. Ernie Suggs, "Mari Copeny: Activist, 11, Is Face, Voice of Flint Water Crisis," *Atlanta Journal-Constitution*, February 28, 2019, https://www.ajc.com/lifestyles/mari-copeny-activist-face-voice-flint-water-crisis/ltBhSYnuS7ViDK6W8DHeeP/.

10. Suggs, "Mari Copeny."

11. "Little Miss Flint Selling T-Shirts: 'Don't Forget Flint.'" *Fox 2 Detroit*, June 1, 2018, https://www.fox2detroit.com/news/little-miss-flint-selling-t-shirts-dont-forget-flint.

12. Suggs, "Mari Copeny."; Katie McBride, "Getting to Work with Little Miss Flint," *Shondaland*, March 22, 2018, https://www.shondaland.com/inspire/a19485789/getting-to-work-with-little-miss-flint/; "Meet the 10-Year-Old Who Donated 1,000 Backpacks to Flint Students," *ABC News*, August 10, 2017, https://abcnews.go.com/Lifestyle/meet-10-year-donated-1000-backpacks-flint-students/story?id=49133870; "8-Year-Old Flint Girl Who Wrote Letter to Obama: 'I Wanted Him to Know What Was Going on,'" *Time*, April 27, 2016, https://time.com/4310492/8-year-old-flint-girl-letter-obama/; Heather Mason, "Meet Smart Girl Mari Copeny aka 'Little Miss Flint,'" *Amy Poehler's Smart Girls*, August 22, 2017, https://amysmartgirls.com/meet-smart-girl-mari-copeny-aka-little-miss-flint-4131419a31bd; Latifah Muhammad, "Little Miss Flint Launches Campaign to Provide Free Bottled Water for Flint Residents," *Vibe*, May 31, 2018, https://www.vibe.com/news/national/little-miss-flint-launches-campaign-to-provide-free-bottled-water-for-flint-residents-588927/; Mary Pauline Lowry, "This Is How One Sixth Grade Girl Helped Improve Flint's Water Crisis," *Oprah Daily*, December 11, 2018, https://www.oprahdaily.com/life/a25383285/mari-copeny-barack-obama-flint-water-crisis/; Maya Richard-Craven, "Is the Water in Flint Finally Safe?" *Sacramento Observer*, March 23, 2023, https://sacobserver.com/2023/03/is-the-water-in-flint-finally-safe/; "Prosecutors Say Court Decision Forces the End of Criminal Cases in Flint Water Scandal," *Associated Press*, October 31, 2023, https://www.npr.org/2023/10/31/1209750922/flint-water-rick-snyder-michigan-prosecution; Chelsea Rose, "Just over 9 Years Later, Does Flint Still Not Have Clean Water?" *WKFR*, May 1, 2023, https://wkfr.com/flint-water-status-2023/

CHAPTER 10

1. James Foster, "From Tear Gas to Tweets: 50 Years in the Evolution of US Activism," *Christian Science Monitor*, July 27, 2018, https://www.csmonitor.com/USA/Society/2018/0727/From-tear-gas-to-tweets-50-years-in-the-evolution-of-US-activism.

2. Megan Carnegie, "Gen Z: How Young People Are Changing Activism," *BBC*, August 8, 2022, https://www.bbc.com/worklife/article/20220803-gen-z-how-young-people-are-changing-activism.

3. Carnegie, "Gen Z."

4. "Licypriya Kangujam Kicks Off Great October March 2019," *Sangai Express*, October 21, 2019, https://www.thesangaiexpress.com/Encyc/2019/10/21/

New-Delhi-Oct-21-Eight-year-old-climate-activist-from-Manipur-Licypriya-Kangujam-kicked-off-the-historic-Great-October-March-2019-today-at-India-Gate-New-Delhi-with-thousands-of-supporters-.amp.html.

5. "Aged 7, Licypriya Kangujam Stands outside Parliament to Urge Prime Minister, MPs to Pass Climate Change Law," *Mirror Now News*, June 22, 2019, https://www.timesnownews.com/mirror-now/society/article/aged-7-licypriya-kangujam-stands-outside-parliament-to-urge-prime-minister-mps-to-pass-climate-change-law/441304; Deepak Lavania, "10-Year-Old Climate Activist Shares Pic of Trash around Taj Mahal," *Times of India*, June 23, 2022, https://timesofindia.indiatimes.com/city/agra/10-yr-old-climate-activist-shares-pics-of-trash-around-taj-mahal/amp_articleshow/92394853.cms; "Climate Activist Lauds Agra Authorities for Clearing Waste from Banks of Yamuna behind Taj," *Hindustan Times*, July 3, 2022, https://www.hindustantimes.com/cities/lucknow-news/climate-activist-lauds-agra-authorities-for-clearing-waste-from-banks-of-yamuna-behind-taj-101656807130997-amp.html; "Tweet of 10-Year-Old Climate Activist Forces Authority to Clean Garbage around Taj Mahal," *India Blooms News Service*, June 24, 2022, https://www.indiablooms.com/health-details/E/11671/tweet-of-10-year-old-climate-activist-forces-authority-to-clean-garbage-around-taj-mahal.html; Lela Nargi, "11-Year-Old Climate Activist Inspires Action through Social Media," *Washington Post*, October 11, 2022, https://www.washingtonpost.com/kidspost/2022/10/11/licypriya-kangujam-kid-climate-activist/.

6. Chase Puentes, "Social Media and Environmental Activism: An Evolving Relationship," School of Marine and Environmental Affairs, College of the Environment, University of Washington, October 18, 2021, https://smea.uw.edu/currents/social-media-and-environmental-activism-an-evolving-relationship.

7. Frank Leon Roberts, "How Black Lives Matter Changed the Way Americans Fight for Freedom," *ACLU News & Commentary*, July 13, 2018, https://www.aclu.org/news/racial-justice/how-black-lives-matter-changed-way-americans-fight; Jonah Kay, "The Evolution of Instagram Activism," *Hyperallergic*, October 31, 2020, https://hyperallergic.com/597846/the-evolution-of-instagram-activism/.

8. Foster, "From Tear Gas to Tweets."

9. John F. Kennedy, "Inaugural Address," *John F. Kennedy Presidential Library and Museum*, https://www.jfklibrary.org/learn/about-jfk/historic-speeches/inaugural-address.

ABOUT THE AUTHOR

JAY RUDERMAN, as a lawyer and international activist, has focused his life's work on seeking social justice by advocating for the rights of people with disabilities worldwide. He is also host of *All About Change*, an award-winning podcast focused on activism, inclusion, and creating change. He lives in the Boston area with his wife, Shira, and their four children.